What Are They Saying About the Social Setting of the New Testament?

Carolyn Osiek, RSCJ

PAULIST PRESS
New York / Ramsey

Library of Congress
Catalog Card Number: 84-60730

ISBN: 0-8091-2625-7

Published by Paulist Press
545 Island Road, Ramsey, N.J. 07446

Printed and bound in the
United States of America

Contents

Contents

*To My Parents,
My First and Lasting Models
of Christian Community*

Introduction

A New Field of Biblical Inquiry

For some years now experts in the social sciences have been turning their attention to one of the richest fields for the study of human group interaction: religion. Similarly, classicists and ancient historians have been investigating for over a century the history, economy, literature, and social life of the Greek and Roman civilizations that flourished on the shores of the Mediterranean Sea in the centuries just before and after the beginning of the Christian era. Meanwhile, back in the Church, theologians and biblicists have been pondering even longer that collection of writings which Jews and Christians hold to be divinely inspired: the Bible. With few exceptions, the three groups continued on their respective ways with little to say to one another.

What has happened in recent years, however, has changed the picture. Scholars in the three fields are now listening to one another more, so that the methods and findings of the social scientists and the researchers of Greco-Roman civilization can be brought to bear on the Bible and, more specifically for our present interest, on the New Testament and the beginnings of the Church.

Underlying this new trend in biblical studies is an important assumption. The Church is both divine and human; the Bible is both word of God and human word. As God's word, it transcends history and culture, as does the Church in its transcendent aspect. But as human word, the Bible is produced by a human Church, subject to the historical vision and cultural patterns of the faith communities and writers which produced it.

1

The more we realize this last assertion and its implications, the more we are aware of the problems it poses. It means that we must always leave open the possibility, often to the point of probability, that a biblical statement comes out of a certain historical and cultural perspective which may or may not be ours.

Between the first and the twentieth centuries there is not only a tremendous expanse of time. The scientific and psychological revolutions that have taken place in the last five hundred years have irreversibly changed the way we (at least we Westerners and those others touched in some way by Western culture) see the world and interpret experience. When I watch the sun move across the sky, I see a fiery ball, the center of our universe, around which our planet revolves. I do not see a golden orb passing through the extended body of the sky goddess Nut as did the ancient Egyptians, or Apollo's golden chariot traveling across the sky as did the Greeks. If I have the misfortune to experience an earthquake, I attribute it to geological disturbances beneath the earth's surface, not to the anger of the god of the underworld. And if I suddenly begin engaging in violent anti-social behavior, I will be confined for psychiatric evaluation, not exorcism, before any judgment is made about responsibility and penalty for my actions.

These simple examples serve to illustrate a complex fact, that we moderns have a totally different way of constructing and interpreting our world than did people of ancient times. So when we translate and interpret the Bible, we necessarily do it in our own terms, in words and concepts familiar to us from our own cultural world. This realization must make us think at least twice before saying that we know with absolute certainty what a biblical passage means.

Does this mean that there is no timeless truth in the Bible, that everything in it is merely cultural conditioning? No, it does not. Because the Bible is God's word, it does contain timeless truth. This truth is expressed *through* the human word, so that the attempt to understand its meaning (exegesis) must always take into account what a text *meant* in its own historical, social, and literary context as well as what it *means* today in ours. To neglect either step is to interpret very inadequately. The social and sociological study of early Christianity can help enormously with the first of these steps. (The difference between social and sociological will be explained below.)

How Did We Get There from Form Criticism?

Those who have followed the evolution of New Testament studies in the last century, or who have even had a good New Testament course in college or graduate school, know that the so-called "historical-critical method," pioneered by Martin Dibelius and Rudolf Bultmann in the early years of this century, has dominated New Testament study. Form criticism seeks to identify literary forms in the text; source criticism isolates literary and oral sources upon which the author has drawn; redaction criticism attends to how the author has worked with his material in order to make his own theological points; historical criticism leads to judgments about the historical reliability of information contained in a text. All of these helpful exercises lead toward one goal: establishing as nearly as possible what the text meant in its own environment.

Now there is the feeling among many scholars that, while these methods are just beginning to be applied to much of the non-canonical literature surrounding both Old and New Testaments, their possibilities have just about been exhausted in regard to the New Testament, and that to gain new insights we need to look at the text through different eyes. Another factor is the increase of social awareness and concern on the part of the Churches, prompting questions about such issues as the economic background of Jesus and the first Christians, their attitudes about family life, the poor, the role of women, etc.

This recent concern about the social framework of the New Testament has earlier precedents in the work of such writers as those of the "Chicago School," Shirley Jackson Case (*Evolution of Early Christianity,* 1914; *The Social Origins of Christianity,* 1923; *The Social Triumph of the Ancient Church,* 1934) and Shailer Matthews (*The Social Teaching of Jesus: An Essay in Christian Sociology,* 1897; *The Atonement and the Social Process,* 1930). Frederick Grant's *Economic Background of the Gospels* (first published 1926; republished N.Y.: Atheneum, 1973) was equally influential and of lasting value. But studies like these were not frequent, and were produced under the influence of this century's first wave of American Christian social concern, which gave way in the 1930's to more dogmatic and ecclesiological pursuits.

Now within the past ten years or so an increasing number of books and articles have appeared on the social context and structure of early Christianity. They hold promise of being the beginning of a new direction in New Testament studies, providing methods which can be used alongside the historical-critical methods to yield fresh insights about the biblical texts and the people who wrote and first read them.

Social and Sociological

Actually we are dealing not with one approach but two, and it is well at this point to make the distinction which is too often blurred even by scholars in the field.

On the one hand, there is social description and analysis, using the findings of archeology (excavations, art, inscriptions, coins), history, and literature contemporary to the texts. Through this method we can gather data and form concepts regarding social life and organization, political life, institutions, social dynamics, and horizons of consciousness. For example, a solid acquaintance with customs of pagan temple sacrifice and the social institution of private banquets in first century Corinth can shed quite a bit of light on Paul's discussion of eating meat offered to idols in 1 Corinthians 8:1–13 and 10:14–33. Again, an investigation of official language of the Roman emperor cult through literary texts, inscriptions, and coins suggests that the readers of Luke 2:10–11 would have read far more political overtones into those simple lines than we do.

On the other hand, the application of social science theory to New Testament texts is quite another thing. This method obviously builds on the other, for without adequate detailed information a sociological analysis would be impossible. Here the constructs of sociologists and cultural or social anthropologists like Max Weber,[1] Ernst Troeltsch,[2] Mary Douglas,[3] Peter Berger,[4] Victor Turner[5] and many others have proved especially helpful to New Testament scholars. Thus for instance Weber's theories about the evolution of a sect into an institution and the consequent changes in the notion of charism have provided one way of interpreting the characteristics of the Pauline churches and the way community structures and "charismatic" gifts seem to be treated differently between the earlier and later letters of the Pauline collection. Or again, Turner's categories of "structure" and "communitas," like Douglas' slightly different "group" and "grid" as complementary poles of individual and communal self-awareness, provide a framework for looking in a new way at the formation of Christian identity and community in the early Church.

The study of the New Testament and early Christianity with social science models presents some serious difficulties. Foremost among them is the obvious fact that social science theories are modern constructions whose users can sometimes forget about the time gap of which we have spoken between us and first century people, and assume in subtle and not so subtle ways that our concepts and theirs are the same. This is where a wise use of social or cultural (British and American terms nearly identical in meaning) anthropology saves the day, for anthropology by its nature is cross-cultural and comparative, and therefore less vulnerable to this pitfall. Another difficulty is that texts from the New Testament and other ancient literature were not written with the purpose of yielding the kind of information which the sociologist primarily seeks: 1 Corinthians was not written as a social description of the Corinthian community but as a pastoral commentary on theological and disciplinary problems; the Gospel of John was not written to describe the relationship of Johannine Christians to the rest of the world but to make strong and uncompromising statements about the identity of Jesus as believed by that community. Yet in both cases, to cite only these two examples, the reader on the lookout for sociological clues must seek them in the texts and whatever other literary or archeological evidence is available, for that is all we have. We must realize that we are working with incomplete evidence.

Still another difficulty is that in the case of biblical texts we are dealing with literature that is not only social but also theological, not only historical but also canonical, that is, authoritative in some way. Theology is one of the most effective ways of structuring life and of giving meaning to experience. In that sense it is matter for sociological analysis. But theology of its nature transcends the social plane and provides means of experiencing that which is beyond what can be perceived and conceived. There is the danger that social and sociological study of early Christianity can take the reductionist approach of limiting religious experience to patterns of group behavior where it can be observed and categorized, rather than recognizing it as the bridge between everyday existence and the Transcendent.

In spite of the potential difficulties which must be constantly kept in mind by scholars using these methods, the social and social science approaches to the New Testament and early Christianity are providing new and valid insights into the life and experience of the first Christians, and, even more important, into how we can today better understand and live their faith.

The following pages are an attempt to summarize some of the principal approaches and discoveries of the social and sociological study of the New Testament. Because this is a rapidly expanding new body of literature, it is impossible to discuss or even mention everything that has been written in the area. For more detailed and evaluative accounts, see some of the summary articles and books that have recently appeared.[6]

> Those of you who have been baptized into Christ
> have put on Christ.
> There is no Jew nor Greek,
> there is no slave nor free,
> there is no male and female,
> for you are all one in Christ Jesus (Gal 3:27–28).

Paul's proclamation of baptismal unity claims to overcome the differences of race, status, and sex which human society imposes. Baptism into the Christian community overcomes these barriers proleptically—that is, we begin in our own history to catch a glimpse of future possibilities. We cannot see the full realization now, but we can look forward to it, and meanwhile seek to implement the vision in our own lives.

Here I am reminded of Mary Daly's statement of many years ago: "In Christ there is neither male nor female. The trouble is, everywhere else there *is!*" What can be said of sexual discrimination can be said as well of race and social status. The baptismal statement used by Paul in the above passage cuts to the heart of differences and divisions in human society. As has always been the case, the people of the

New Testament brought their own cultural experience with its patterns of perception and behavior with them into the Church. As Christians they continued to see the world as people of their own time. It is this world of the first century Mediterranean culture that we will now explore.

Part I
JEW AND GREEK:
MERGING CULTURES

1
Judaism and Hellenism
in the First Century

It is not the purpose of this volume to give an account of historical events. For historical accounts the reader is referred to the appropriate sections in books on New Testament background, of which there are many, or to F.F. Bruce, *New Testament History* or Bo Reicke, *The New Testament Era,* whole volumes devoted to the history of the period just before and after the time of New Testament events. What will be discussed here are recent findings with regard to social and cultural interaction during that time.

We are speaking here of "Judaism" and "Hellenism." Most readers will be reasonably sure they know what is meant by Judaism: a religious tradition and cultural grouping existing from ancient times, historically connected with the land of Palestine, and characterized by a strong monotheistic faith based on that part of the Bible which Christians are accustomed to call the Old Testament. With that broad a definition probably any Jewish groups in the ancient world would have agreed, but the varieties of Jewish religion and culture in the Roman Empire were equally as varied as they are today. A Pharisee in Jerusalem and a philosophical writer in the Diaspora like Philo of Alexandria may have had very little in common in regard to lifestyle, piety, or interpretation of the Scriptures. What they would have uncompromisingly agreed upon, however, is the legacy of those Scriptures to testify to God's continuing covenant with Israel.

Our second term "Hellenism" may need more explanation. The classical Greek culture of earlier centuries was taking on new forms in the late fourth century BCE, just at the time of a movement that was to change the face of the eastern Mediterranean world. The Macedonians in the northern mountains of Greece under the leadership of Alexander the Great began a military expansion to the East to subdue the Persian Empire and open the way to India. In their wake came Greek, or Hellenistic, culture. When Alexander died suddenly in Persia at the height of his career in 323 BCE, his generals divided up the eastern Mediterranean from Greece all the way to Egypt into empires for themselves, Greek empires in which government, economics, and culture were syncretized into a new kind of civilization that was to be adapted later by the Romans and remain the dominant culture in the eastern Mediterranean world until the Arab conquest of the seventh century.

In Palestine and in Diaspora Jewish communities elsewhere, Jewish and Hellenistic culture came into direct contact and in some cases conflict. When two cultures meet, elements of each are retained, dropped, or transformed. This kind of phenomenon has been continually studied by sociologists and anthropologists and is continually occurring. One need only remember the "melting pot" of nineteenth century American immigration or observe what is happening today with new waves of immigrants. In the case of the immigrants, the challenge is adapting to a local dominant culture into which they are plunged. To better understand the analogy to the ancient world and Hellenism, we need to observe how the resident or local culture is affected by the new arrivals: the influence of African music on jazz, the necessity for bilingualism in southern Florida or California, etc.

The older cultures of the Ancient Near East, that of the Jews in Palestine among them, were now beset with invader-conquerors who brought their own language, dress, lifestyle, religion, government, taxation systems, and manufactured products, and proceeded to impose them on the local population. First experienced in its economic and political effects, Hellenism became within a century the culture of the upper classes in the whole eastern Mediterranean.

After military occupation came civil government structures with their particularly hated aspect of taxation, administered by the method that remained in force through Roman times: tax farming—

government concession of the right to collect taxes within a given area. Whether property taxes, poll taxes, sales or road use taxes, all were generally collected by agents hated not only for their immediate role, but also as representatives of a foreign occupying power except from about 134 to 64 BCE during the Jewish Hasmonean monarchy.

More subtle Greek influence followed. Many of the Jerusalem aristocracy realized that under this regime the only way to prosper was to adopt certain aspects of Greek culture: language, dress, participation in the leisure activities of theatre and athletics, assuming Greek names and giving them to their children. Some of this is described in 1 Maccabees 1:11–15 and 2 Maccabees 4:10–15 through events of about 170 BCE, especially the aristocracy building a gymnasium and sending their sons to compete in athletic contests, even going to the point of undergoing plastic surgery to remove the sign of circumcision so they would not be ridiculed by their Greek companions. Notice that in both accounts it is Jews, not foreigners, who initiate these events. In this case they are not being imposed upon directly by their pagan occupiers.

This is not to say that there was no pressure to conform. Cultured Greeks of the period tended to see themselves as racially and culturally superior to "barbarians" (everyone else), who then felt it necessary to prove themselves by demonstrating how Greek they could be.

To stricter Jews, however, these kinds of changes meant compromise and apostasy from the Jewish faith, for it was impossible to live like a Greek and observe the Law in its full rigor, just as it was virtually impossible to frequent theatre, baths, and gymnasium without being associated with Greek religion in the form of public prayer and sacrifice. Moreover, the exposure of the body required for bathing at the public baths and competing nude at the gymnasium was considered morally reprehensible. During the first century of Greek rule under the Ptolemies of Egypt, there was less pressure, less direct interference in local affairs in Palestine. But after the country was taken over by a rival dynasty, the Seleucids from Antioch about 200 BCE, more direct policies of Hellenization were pursued. It was the clash between this and the older culture in Palestine, and specifically the intended "reform" by the "enlightened" Hellenized Jerusalem aristocrats, encouraged and sanctioned by the rather naive Seleucid king

Antiochus Epiphanes, which provoked the Maccabean revolt of the 160's BCE, the story of which is narrated in 1 and 2 Maccabees.

The Maccabean war was the beginning of the re-establishment of home rule under the Hasmonean dynasty until that monarchy was usurped by Herod the Great in 40 BCE. But rather than being the end of Hellenism, it was only the beginning. The Hasmoneans continued to be quite influenced by it in culture, if not in religion. Historical and archeological evidence, some only recently brought to light, indicates that Herod's remodeling of Jerusalem and the Temple turned them into magnificent showplaces in Greco-Roman style, so that the Jerusalem Jesus knew was not that of today's Old City with its narrow winding medieval streets, but a city in stone and marble with a sixty foot wide main street and graceful columned porticoes. Herod was also responsible for the splendid new seaport of Caesarea on the coast, later seat of Roman administration, an entirely new Roman city which was to be a significant location for both Peter (Acts 10) and Paul (Acts 23:23—26:23).[1]

Most of this information has been known all along, of course, for it is part of the biblical literature and the *Antiquities* of the first century historian Josephus. It has been customary to look at the clash between Judaism and Hellenism in Palestine in the Hellenistic period as simply one of two cultures, that of the conquered and that of the conquerors, with a minimum of intermingling and a great deal of resistance on the part of the conquered.

In view of more careful study of the literature and archeological evidence and some comparative study of other similar situations, several new approaches have come to light.

It is too simple to see this encounter as that of two competing cultures, but we can understand its dynamics much better if we can see it in terms of tradition and modernity. Some people collect antiques, others collect video games. Typically, the older generation generally prefers to do things "the way they've always been done," whether in communications, interior decoration, shopping, entertainment, or that last bastion of permanence—religion. Just as typically, the younger generation is generally more open to change because they haven't yet become familiar with definite ways of circumscribing culture.

Those who want to get ahead economically and socially will migrate to the occupations and social circles where they think this is possible—computer science, the sunbelt jetset, etc. Those optimistic about progress see unlimited possibilities for the future. Those concerned about tradition and its values wonder if progress isn't betrayal. In a technological age, can science, the new religion, preserve the respect for human and family life upon which our civilization is built? Can progress and truth co-exist?

To broaden the picture a bit, let us consider today's Middle East, a region as wrenched by conflict today as it was twenty centuries ago. For the strictly observant Moslem or Jew, tradition means fidelity to ancestral faith as it has been conveyed within a cultural context, including in both cases certain ways of dressing, public behavior, restriction of women to household roles, etc. But to advance socially and economically, today's Jewish or Moslem young adult must learn English, and with knowledge of the language comes exposure to a whole new world of consumerism and values alien to the traditional way of life and belief. Dressing modernly seems immodest, the sensual bombardment of the media creates different ways of relating, public roles for women are seen as a threat to the sacredness of the family and its values. Can the strength of tradition be retained if the new ways are adopted? The popularity of conservative movements both in Orthodox Israeli Judaism and in the Moslem countries is clearly saying that for many, including the young, the answer is a resounding *no*.

These are questions very similar to those asked by the sincerely religious Palestinian Jew of the mid-second century BCE. And what is important for our interests, the same questions were still being asked by the contemporaries of Jesus and Paul.

Palestinian and Hellenistic Judaism

Another new approach concerns the difference between so-called Palestinian Judaism and Hellenistic Judaism. By New Testament times there had been considerable colonies of Jews outside Palestine for at least six hundred years, particularly in Egypt, and presumably longer than that in Babylonia. These Diaspora Jews in the Mediterranean area found themselves after Alexander's conquest living in an increasingly Hellenized environment without the support of home city,

Temple, and majority population enjoyed by the Jews of Palestine. In the urban centers of Egypt, North Africa, Syria, and Asia Minor, they found themselves in a Greek world to which they more readily adapted. It was in Egypt at least by the third century BCE that the Hebrew Scriptures were translated into Greek, presumably because not all in the congregation understood Hebrew. Diaspora Jews began quite early to give Greek names to their children and generally assimilate themselves as much as possible to their environment while at the same time remaining faithful to the religion of Moses and Abraham.

It had been customary for scholars to assume that Palestinian Judaism remained somehow less tainted with Hellenism, while Diaspora Judaism alone could properly be called Hellenistic. Recently the thorough and monumental research of Martin Hengel has established a different picture. In his two-volume work, *Judaism and Hellenism,* followed later by the smaller *Jews, Greeks, and Barbarians,* Hengel has persuasively shown through painstaking examination of literary, archeological, and inscriptional evidence that from as early as the middle of the third century BCE, a meaningful distinction cannot be made between Palestinian and Hellenistic Judaism. Rather, Hellenism had already by that time so pervaded daily life that Palestinian Jews differed little from their brothers and sisters in the Diaspora in their outlook and the effects of Greek economic, administrative, and cultural influence in their lives, even if their native language was not Greek. Instead of distinguishing between Palestinian and Hellenistic (Diaspora) Judaism, Hengel maintains, we can make a distinction between the Greek-*speaking* Judaism of the Diaspora west of Palestine, and the Aramaic/Hebrew *speaking* Judaism of Palestine and Babylonia. All of it is profoundly influenced by Greek civilization and culture, even in unacknowledged ways.

Thus for instance, the Wisdom literary tradition, already on the way toward philosophical meditation in such books as Job and Proverbs, found familiar ground in Hellenistic literature, particularly popular Stoicism. By equating Wisdom with Torah, the Law (see Ps 119), both as way of life and personified guide (see Prv 8—9; Sir 24), the Jewish Wisdom tradition was able to maintain credibility in cultured circles among admirers of Greek philosophical writings. Books like Qoheleth (Ecclesiastes) and Ben Sira (Ecclesiasticus), though very different, are examples.[2] The exact nature of Greek philosophical influence on Jewish Wisdom literature has always been impossible to make precise, but it is generally accepted that well before the writing of the New Testament, the process had already taken shape.

Less conscious borrowers, but borrowers all the same, Hengel suggests, are the Essenes, the separatist group responsible for the Dead Sea Scrolls at their Qumran monastery. Going with an already recognized theory of their origins in about 150 BCE in reaction to Temple policies with which they were in disagreement, he suggests that their strict and communitarian organization and their totally confident claim to be the only legitimate representatives of authentic Judaism are matched only by the much earlier conventicles of Pythagorean philosophers, known for their asceticism and communal adherence.

Moreover, the external forms and organization of the community closely resemble those of Hellenistic private religious associations, a type of organization apparently unknown previously in Judaism. While wisely rejecting suggestions by earlier scholars of direct borrowing of Hellenistic forms of religious organization by the Jewish purist Essenes, Hengel maintains that without realizing it, and against their best intentions, even the Essenes were caught up on at least the fringes of the Hellenistic cloak.[3]

In spite of his sweeping statements about the overall effects of Hellenism in Palestine, Hengel is careful to say that he is speaking mostly of the aristocratic classes of Jerusalem when considering the greatest influence of Greek language, literature, and leisure. Unfortunately it is the leisured urban classes throughout the ancient world which left the best records of themselves, for it was they who had the education, time, and money to do so. In the areas of trade, taxation, and government, however, the effects of Hellenism were all-pervasive.

Galilee

For some perspectives on what was happening elsewhere than in Jerusalem, we must turn to the second recent major study of Palestine, Sean Freyne's *Galilee from Alexander the Great to Hadrian, 323 B.C.E. to 135 C.E.* It too has been well received by scholars in the field. In contrast to the sophisticated urban environment described by Hengel, Freyne pulls together all the evidence available from literary and archeological sources to portray quite a different picture in the upper regions of Palestine than in the south.

Freyne challenges the interpretation of Isaiah 8:23 (or 9:1), "Galilee of the Gentiles," as indicating that in the post-exilic period there was heavy Gentile settlement in Galilee, creating a quite mixed population. Rather, after examining all the evidence available, he concludes that in the Hellenistic period and into Roman (New Testament) times, Galilee remained a largely Jewish peasant society, with most of the population residing in rural areas and villages.

Even the two major urban centers, Sepphoris in the central plain and Tiberias on the west coast of the Lake of Gennesaret, remained according to Freyne primarily Jewish, though more Hellenized in culture than the rural areas and including Gentile, mostly Greek, minorities. Similarly, the nearby Greek cities of the Decapolis, mostly on the east side of the Jordan, probably had Jewish minorities.

Sepphoris and Tiberias were both new cities in New Testament times, rebuilt in one case and built anew (over a cemetery!) in the other, both by Herod Antipas, the Herod of the Gospel Passion narratives. Both were administrative capitals at one time and stood in some rivalry with one another. While Sepphoris is no longer inhabited, the modern city of Tiberias gives one something of the impression that the ancient city must have conveyed, built near a hot springs spa, sprawling down the hills to the lake at its feet, visible from any point on the lake—a vacation spot in a splendid location.

The cities had a Greek form of city government, a Greek way of life, and were therefore treated with some hostility by the rural population. Significantly, the Gospels never indicate that Jesus even entered either one. In the revolt against Rome, 66-70 CE, Sepphoris remained loyal to Rome, true to its Hellenizing tendencies, while Tiberias entered the war half-heartedly, with a populace very divided on the question. It was subdued by the Roman general Vespasian, but treated not unkindly by the Roman conquerors.[4]

The Galilean towns of which we hear in the Gospels—Nazareth, Bethsaida, Capernaum, Magdala, Cana, and Chorazim—were probably villages in comparison, though Bethsaida, Capernaum, and Magdala all lay along the principal road from the Mediterranean to Damascus in Roman times, and must therefore have done a brisk business in trade and supplies. Magdala (Aramaic for "tower") had an alternate name not mentioned in the Gospels, Taricheae (Greek for "salted fish"), perhaps an indication of the base of its lakeside economy.

While small ancestral peasant holdings were still the basis of land allotment in Galilee in New Testament times, increasingly the best land was held in royal estates, parcelled out to whomever the prevailing occupiers wished to reward, confiscated and reallotted when its owners fell out of favor with the crown. Thus large stretches of land worked by tenant farmers were owned and administered from the urban centers, whence came also the tax farmers. The country people of Galilee experienced the effects of Hellenization in ways that did not make them well disposed to its benefits. They retained a firm and abiding loyalty to the spiritual significance of Jerusalem with its Temple worship, and held more in common with the older, traditional way of life inasmuch as it could still be found in Jerusalem, than with the cities closer to them. The peasants of Galilee must have been the backbone of the traditional pilgrimages to Jerusalem for the great feasts (cf. Lk 2:41; Jn 2:23; 5:1; 7:2, 10; 11:55).

What languages were spoken in Palestine at the time of Jesus? After half a century of Roman occupation, the legal language was Latin, but since apparently so few really understood it, most official documents and decrees were also promulgated in Greek. After three centuries of Hellenistic administration and commerce, the commercial language was predominantly Greek. Even most of the country people must have understood at least business and "tourist" Greek. Consider Jesus' numerous encounters with non-Jews in the Gospels, from the citizens of the Greek Decapolis city Gadara or Gerasa (Mt 8:28–34; Mk 5:1–20; Lk 8:26–39) to the Roman governor Pilate in the Passion narratives. Freyne rightly raises the question whether language of itself changes thought patterns, even if there is a concerted effort to prevent it. But since the Persian conquest of the sixth century BCE, Aramaic had replaced Hebrew as the everyday language of the ordinary people, and it probably remained so in rural areas and among the lower classes of the cities as well. Those who attended Temple or synagogue services in Palestine, except for "Hellenist" synagogues in Jerusalem for Diaspora visitors and immigrants (Acts 6:1; 9:29), heard the Scripture reading in Hebrew, and could perhaps even speak it somewhat for formal occasions.[5]

In Palestine during New Testament times, then, the large cities represented centers of Greco-Roman culture and at the same time political and economic power. Jerusalem, Caesarea, Tiberias, and Sepphoris were modern centers of progress where communication with and recognition from the larger world of the Roman Empire was highly valued. Here the still predominantly Jewish populations saw less difficulty combining Greek speech, dress, and lifestyle with their ancestral religious traditions than did many of their fellow Jews of the villages and countryside who were, quite simply, far less likely to benefit from Hellenism and more likely to be oppressed by it because of the prevailing economic and social system.

The Diaspora

What can be said of Jewish Hellenization in the Diaspora? This is an immense topic covering a much larger range chronologically, geographically, and demographically, and could never be covered in a single study. Hengel's second work on the topic, *Jews, Greeks, and Barbarians,* gives a brief but solid introduction.[6] In areas where there were large Jewish communities and where sufficient evidence remains, we see a number of different trends happening.

Jewish Diaspora communities were usually cohesively organized around synagogue groupings that may have been based on neighborhood or national origin or both, sometimes with an overall *gerousia* or council of elders, for the entire Jewish population of the city, as in Alexandria. In this way they modeled their group identity as a *politeuma* or assembly of citizens within a city on the larger identity of the Greek citizens of the city as a whole. They were a city within a city. When the Jewish population of a city grew very large as in Alexandria (a third of the population in the first and second centuries CE) this could cause friction which would result in discrimination, oppression, and revolt, as indeed it did there several times during that period.

As could be expected, Jewish communities in Greek-speaking environments inevitably assimilated to Hellenistic culture, and apparently with much less strain than in Palestine. One of the obvious signs is adoption of Greek and later Latin names, just as in the somewhat later evidence of the Jews of Rome, known through funerary inscriptions, the same trend can be traced from one generation to the next, moving not from Jewish to Greek but now from Greek to Latin names.[7] Other indications include use of the Greek Bible, and the increasing influence of Greek literary and philosophical traditions on Jewish writers, especially the great philosopher Philo of Alexandria, a contemporary of Paul.[8] This assimilation happened generally in one direction only, toward Hellenism, rather than toward the older native cultures, Egyptians in Alexandria, Syrians in Antioch, etc. It followed the pattern usually found in situations where a new, modern, dominant culture points the way toward social advancement. The older cultures often get their revenge, however, particularly through influence on popular religion, magic, and superstition.

Thus another trend is also observable especially in Diaspora communities: the attraction of non-Jews to certain aspects of Jewish religion, especially its strict monotheism and strong ethical standards, so that in many urban areas a steady stream of non-Jews, including Greeks and Romans, became attracted to synagogue worship and eventually attached themselves to the Jewish community, either as proselytes who took upon themselves full observance of the Law (see Acts 13:43), or as interested frequenters who maintained a looser relationship. It is probably this latter group who are referred to in Acts 13:50; 16:14; 17:4, 17; 18:7, though it is disputed whether "God-fearers" is a technical synagogue term or not. In the late first century something of a public scandal was created in Rome when several members of one of the best aristocratic families closely connected to the emperor Domitian himself were accused of adopting Jewish customs. Two hundred years later the Church historian Eusebius claimed that they were really Christians; they may have been converts to a still quite Jewish form of Christianity, which we know continued for several centuries.

Conclusion and Implications for the New Testament

Recent investigation of the meeting of Jewish and Hellenistic culture in the formative centuries before the New Testament era has shown that in Palestine as in the Diaspora, at a very early stage the urban Jews were deeply affected by Hellenism, so that the conventional distinction between Palestinian and Hellenistic (Diaspora) Judaism is no longer viable.

In Palestine Greek culture was experienced at the beginning of the Hellenistic period just after the conquest by Alexander the Great first in its military, political, and economic effects. The introduction of Hellenistic systems of administration and taxation deepened the rift between urban aristocratic landholders and tax farmers on one side who stood to benefit by increasing involvement in the Hellenistic world, and the rural peasantry who were largely its victims on the other. Hellenism, always an urban culture, rewarded the upwardly-mobile city dweller at the expense of the rural population who therefore remained more loyal to traditional ways of life. These tendencies were true throughout the Greek East, not only in Palestine.

In the Diaspora, Jewish communities attained a remarkable amount of cohesiveness in some of the large cities, while their assimilation to Hellenism went more smoothly in most cases. Synagogues were for the most part open centers of worship which attracted non-Jews.

In the first part of the Hellenistic era, Greek purism from earlier years remained a source of at least an ideological division between those of Greek birth, language, and culture, and the rest of humanity, grouped together uncritically as barbarians. In the early years of Roman expansion, even the Romans were considered barbarians by the Greek literary aristocracy.

There were challenges to this view, however. Already Alexander saw himself as creator of a cosmopolis, a world-city. In the first and second centuries BCE, more change of perspective was brought about under the influence of the Stoic philosophers' concept of the world community, a common human unity, brought together of course by a common language and culture, that of Hellenism.[9] While Greek culture was clearly superior, now presumably everyone could aspire to it. It was this philosophical movement toward a human community as well as the common economic and social community created by the expansion of Hellenistic power and culture in the eastern Mediterranean which facilitated Roman imperial expansion in the first century BCE and ultimately the rapid spread of Christianity in the following centuries, for it was into this world of Hellenistic urban culture that Paul and his fellow missionaries went forth to proclaim the Gospel.

At this point Paul's proclamation in Gal 3:28 and Rom 10:12 (but see the puzzling variation in Colossians 3:11) that there is neither

Jew nor Greek in Christ must mean far more in light of what we have seen in the preceding pages. It should be clear by now that all of these events carry tremendous implications for our reading of the New Testament. If we are to understand its message within the context of the writers' own world, we must know something of that world, which these pages have attempted to sketch.

One important result is that we cannot facilely try to divide what is "Greek" from what is "Jewish" in New Testament literature, as writers sometimes enjoy doing. To use an example: in the prologue of John's Gospel, Jesus is spoken of as the Word, or Logos in Greek. Much ink has been spilled trying to decide whether John's use of the concept comes from Greek Stoic philosophy *or* Jewish Wisdom literature. The answer in light of recent scholarship on Hellenism and Judaism is: both together. Or again, the question arises whether the first generation of Christians in urban centers like Antioch and Corinth understood the Eucharist along the model of Jewish table fellowship meals *or* Hellenistic banquets. Again, the answer has to be some of both.

Another factor to bear in mind is the difference between rural and urban life in the eastern Mediterranean, even to the point of hostility in some cases. This is a point acknowledged but not sufficiently developed by Hengel in his vigorous assertions about the extent of Hellenism in Palestine. It receives more attention from Freyne, but his focus is on Galilee, so that the rural-urban tension in Judea and other parts of Palestine has not really been studied. While Jesus and most of his followers came from Galilean village life, Matthew/Levi the tax collector may have represented an entirely different constituency, and the seven appointed to assist the apostles (Acts 6) in the early Jerusalem years are all men with Greek names serving in large part Greek-speaking Jewish Christians. The rural Palestinian roots of Christianity sprang quickly into an urban thicket. But more of this in Chapter 2.

2
First Century Consciousness

Now that we have considered some of the social factors in the first century Mediterranean world in their historical setting, it will be enlightening to approach that world from another angle, that of models from the social sciences.

As mentioned earlier, we in the twentieth century West live in an entirely different world of meaning than did the people of the New Testament. The point of difference began to widen sharply in the modern era with new inventions that revolutionized communications (the printing press), warfare (gun powder), and travel (the steam engine). Enlightenment philosophy probed the value of individualism. Modern technology creates for us a world of virtually unlimited knowledge, storage and retrieval of information, and even (some would say) unlimited economic growth.

The democratic and capitalist principles teach us that at least theoretically the individual's right to "life, liberty, and the pursuit of happiness" is supreme, that independence and self-reliance are praiseworthy, and that the possibility of advancement resulting from hard work is limitless (though it is precisely disillusionment with these lofty promises that is causing much of today's social upheaval). The psychological revolution begun by Freud's and Jung's adventures into the previously uncharted unconscious reveals to us another frontier whose limit has yet to be sighted. In short, apart from occasional setbacks and the threat of nuclear disaster, the assumptions on which our society operates are those of limitless horizons and the value of the individual over against society. The imposing of limits, whether by economic policy, legislation, or unequal opportunity, is precisely what provokes rebellion of one kind or another.

The sociologist or anthropologist and the biblical scholar are together vividly aware of one major reality: we cannot go back. There is no way that we as twentieth century Westerners can completely shed our assumptions and horizon of experience and take on the mindset of a person who has had no exposure to our culture. This of course poses a serious problem for our understanding of the Bible, as we already saw in the introduction. What we can do, however, is to make use of the comparative models provided by the social sciences, in this case cultural anthropology which studies patterns of social behavior across many cultures.

Recently Bruce J. Malina has admirably set out such a selection of models in *The New Testament World: Insights from Cultural Anthropology*. Intended as a college text, the book is highly readable and packed with amusing and apt contemporary examples to illustrate its principles. Let us together briefly examine the categories of first century consciousness as he presents them, under the image of eavesdropping on a group of foreigners, the people of the New Testament.

Honor and Shame

After a methodological introduction, chapter 2 is devoted to honor and shame, what Malina calls the "pivotal values" of the New Testament world. Honor comprises two essential and complementary elements: the claim of worth and recognition of that worth by significant others. "Ascribed honor" is that prestige and status which comes with birth, the most secure kind of honor in the ancient world. "Acquired honor" is that esteem earned by an individual or group by deeds of heroism or benevolence. Honor is recognition in three major areas: power, sexual status, and religion, that is, appropriate ability to control others, appropriate male/female roles, and appropriate relationship in the fixed hierarchy of superiors and subordinates, from one's social inferiors all the way to God at the top of the ladder.

Individual honor must be claimed and jealously guarded by the person; collective honor is safeguarded by a head figure, the one at the top of the hierarchy in a particular subset of the social system: the father of a family, the emperor for the empire, etc. In an "agonistic" culture, every interaction outside one's circle of familiars is a contest for honor, a challenge which must be met at the risk of loss of honor. Shame, on the other side, is not so much disgrace as it is a proper sensitivity toward one's own honor, and thus is a positive symbol.

The important points to be recognized if we are to really understand how the system works are twofold. First, it is not enough to know one's worth for oneself; it must also be publicly acknowledged. This aspect has been repeatedly brought to light in the examination of other issues, for instance customs of charity and public aid. Ancient authors who write on the subject will straightforwardly say that one of the major motivations for giving to the poor is the public gratitude and recognition of generosity that results.[1] Gospel injunctions like Matthew 6:2–8, though rooted in rabbinic traditions, were truly countercultural, less so in a Jewish than a Greco-Roman milieu; but remember that in New Testament times, this distinction must be made with great caution. (Notice, though, that the contrasting behavior is that of Gentiles—v. 7.)

The second important point is that honor is the greatest social value, to be preferred over wealth and even life itself. Without a good reputation, life has no meaning. Here as at many points in this discussion it will be helpful to realize that the consciousness we are describing is not only of the past but rather not of the modern Western world. As I write, the PLO in West Beirut are under seige by Israeli forces. Asked by a reporter whether he would prefer reason (surrender and survival) or death with honor, a fifteen year old Palestinian soldier replies: "There is no alternative. If we lose our identity, we lose everything. . . . I would choose honor first. . . ." His brother adds: "I would never place logic before dignity."[2]

Individual and Group

Chapter 3 of Malina's book deals with another important set of alternatives, the relationship of the individual person to his or her social structures. While the modern Westerner may see development of conscience as the ability to responsibly withstand outside forces and proceed instead on one's own sense of right and wrong independently of social pressure, the first century person would rather explain conscience as the coherence of one's public image with the personal self-

image. It is important that one's own self-perception match the perception of significant others.

This description should be borne in mind when reading what Paul
has to say about *syneidēsis,* conscience, a favorite term (see Rom 2:15;
9:1; 13:5; 1 Cor 8:7; 10:25; 2 Cor 1:12; 5:11, etc.) Here Malina appropriately brings in a point raised many years ago by Krister Stendahl
in an important article on Pauline interpretation.[3] In spite of Paul's
language in Romans 7:21–23, which has been enormously misunderstood to make him sound like one possessed of a modern "guilty conscience," personal guilt is really not what Paul is talking about at all.
It is rather his own self-awareness before God *and* how it matches his
standing in the Christian churches that concern him.

Malina suggests that few people today bother to read any first
century writings outside the New Testament because they find them
boring. The reason for this is that the concerns of ancient people were
very different from ours. Both writers and intended readers were asking different questions than we are. Our questions tend to be psychological and individual, largely because we are inheritors of a long tradition of individualism and more recently of "pop-psychology." It is
probable that the people of the ancient world did not know each other
as we do, that is, psychologically, and that therefore terms like "relationship" and "intimacy" would have meant something quite different
to them than to us. Whereas we function day after day with a basic
assumption of the autonomy of individuals, first century Mediterranean people lived with the assumption of the necessary and natural
inherence of persons in their society. As opposed to our individualism
or monadism, this is what the social sciences sometimes call "dyad-
ism," the continual need of another in order to know one's own
identity.

The dyadic person is constantly aware of inter-relationship with
others as a necessary component of self-awareness and self-possession.
One's position in a society both horizontally (in peer relationships) and
vertically (with those of superior and inferior status) are crucial to
self-perception. As we shall see in Chapter 3, this need for a firmly
established structure of social status had a significant influence on the
development of early Christianity. While for the modern "monadic"
person the problem of growth is effective movement outside oneself
into satisfying relationships, the problem for the dyadic person is the

opposite: how can individuation come about, how can a person assert himself or herself over against the social grouping?

In such a society moral norms are set by and for the group to which the individual belongs and conforms. Thus responsibility for morality, stability, security, and harmony rests with the whole community. It follows then that the good of the whole has priority over the good of the individual when these principles come into conflict, for it is the identity and honor of the state, community, and family that must be upheld; the honor of the individual person has meaning only insofar as he or she is a member of those groupings.

As conclusion to this chapter, Malina presents what he calls a "three-zone model" of the dyadic personality, illustrated by many examples from biblical literature. The three zones correspond roughly though not exactly to three areas of human function and behavior as we would see them. The first zone of "emotion-fused thought" includes essentially the inner process of reflection and feeling, expressed in language of the heart, perceptible only in the eyes. The second zone of "self-expressive speech" includes the areas of communication through speech and hearing, thus clustered around the functions of mouth and ears. The third zone of "purposeful action" includes execution of intention and feeling in external movement, and is thus expressed in the functions of hands and feet. Malina suggests that this model of translating human awareness into action was an implicit pattern in which people moved and expressed themselves, and that a writer who uses the language of all three zones is implying the full range of human experience and behavior. Since language about God is largely based on the analogy of human experience, the same three-zone model is often employed to speak about divine intention and action.[4]

A problem arises here in that most of the examples given by Malina are from the Old Testament and therefore a Semitic rather than Greco-Roman context, so that we are again thrown back on the Jewish vs. Greek dichotomy discussed in the previous chapter. It is certainly true that a statement from Exodus or Deuteronomy represents a different cultural world from that of Matthew or Revelation because of the Hellenistic revolution that has happened in between. Yet the same three-zone model seems to be operating in both. Citation of some examples from non-biblical literature of the first century world would have been helpful to demonstrate continuity. But again let us recall all that has been said in the last chapter about the merging of Jewish and Greek culture just before the New Testament era. It seems safe to say that the differences between Jewish and Greek ways of thinking and acting are far less significant than those between the first century dyadic personality and the twentieth century monadic one.

Limited Good

Chapter 4 of Malina's book discusses another category from the social sciences that is very helpful for understanding the differences between the New Testament world and ours, this time an economic concept. The first century Mediterranean world is a fine example of a "classic peasant society: a set of villages socially bound up with preindustrial cities." These cities are population centers which depend on their outlying areas for basic commodities of food and clothing. The dependent country areas, in return, rely on the cities as market centers for their produce and places where manufactured and imported goods are available. Manufacturing is for the most part a small local affair: a family works together at a trade, or a more prosperous manufacturer employs a limited number of people in his workshop. In either case the tradesman-owner sells directly to the customer without intermediary agents. There are exceptions, of course: the merchant of imported goods or, in the Roman period, large brick factories under imperial or aristocratic ownership. Likewise the predominant farming model is the family farm or small farming establishment with direct marketing in an accessible city,[5] though again the vast estates of aristocrats and the feeding of a large populace like that of Rome, Antioch, or Alexandria operated on a larger and less personal scale.

In this model of peasant society and preindustrial cities, there is normally a social stratification into four categories: urban elites, urban non-elites, villagers, and a marginal class composed of beggars and slaves. The urban elite are the only ones with the income and leisure for advanced education and literary output, and hence are the bearers of a society's traditions and standards. Moreover, it is they who control religious institutions, tax structures, and legal systems and who therefore exercise an enormous amount of social power.

Because of this controlling position of the urban elite, new move-ments generally begin with them and work their way down the social scale. Christianity, however, begins with the villager class, and within the first generation after the death of Jesus it has worked its way effec-tively into the urban non-elite group, where it continues to reside until the third century. Indeed Christianity remained an essentially urban religion until the Middle Ages.

I think it is important here to make a distinction between intel-lectual and devotional or enthusiastic movements (my own terms). It can certainly be said that in ancient societies intellectual movements originate among the urban elite, so that intellectually their circles are "where it's at," and other groups below them in the social hierarchy are always somewhat out of step or old-fashioned in comparison. The same need not always be said of movements, particularly religious ones, with a more devotional content; take for example the great pop-ularity of oriental mystery religions in the first centuries of the Chris-tian era. The social dynamic of the movement of Christianity has often been compared to that of these intensely missionary religions which made their way across the empire, giving new meaning and hope for salvation predominantly to the urban non-elite.[6]

In this society consisting mostly of closed, inward-looking systems of village, city, and empire, the vast majority of the population see themselves as severely limited by the social structure, as indeed they are. They are limited as well by the amount of material goods avail-able to them. In a world with neither mass production nor the expand-ing horizons made possible by modern technology, any acquisition, any improvement in status is at someone else's expense. To avoid being on the wrong end of that movement necessitates the cultivation of social and economic stability. Therefore alliances of all kinds are important to ensure that stability; hence the complex system of hori-zontal and vertical reciprocal relationships that grew up in ancient Mediterranean society, and that was so essential to the smooth func-tioning of society. Everyday life was built upon a vast network of patron-client relationships which enabled the less powerful and lower in status to know from whence came their protection, while it gave to the more powerful and higher in status a base of loyal support and an outlet for the generosity which was essential to the social image of their honor.

Such a society based on a perception of limited goods is almost completely without motivation by work ethic, since status based on birth precludes advancement through work. Though there are some exceptions to this economic determinism in the great Roman urban centers, it remains true throughout the empire for the vast majority of people. The poor are not those without money but those deprived of honor by being unable to maintain their inherited status, made so less often by financial disaster than by political or social disgrace.

Kinship and Marriage

Chapter 5 of Malina's book examines patterns and norms that regulate human life in relationship bound up with the life cycle of birth and death, especially as they are revealed in four areas: selection of marriage partners; the marriage bond; immediate family; extended family.

The Mediterranean family was a cohesive unit, a producing as well as consuming center. Its patriarchal authority ruled over an extended system of status structures with strong emphasis on patrilineal continuity, often with definite preference for marriage within the patrilineal extended family. In such a family marriage is not a romantic choice but an institution carefully planned to further the interests of the clan. Recreational groupings are by sex, men with men and women with women, "two exclusive circles that might touch but never overlap." To see this custom still operative, one need only walk through a small town in any Eastern Mediterranean country today in the early evening to find the men gathered in the local cafe while women sit in family and neighborhood groups in yards and on doorsteps exchanging conversation over their needlework.

In such close family units, bonds of loyalty are intense and members wish to remain closely localized. Honor too is a family affair, the responsibility of the patriarchal head or his male representatives to enforce and if necessary avenge. The brother-sister relationship is a primary mode of perpetuating the intense and protective loyalty of family members for one another and for the common honor of the family.

Because most of the examples in this chapter are taken from the Old Testament, it is again, like Chapter 2, less directly helpful for

New Testament study. We will however return to some of the concepts from this chapter in Chapter 6 below when considering the household codes of the later Pauline writings.

Clean and Unclean

The final chapter from Malina's *The New Testament World* we will briefly consider because of the enormous impact of the categories of clean and unclean in the ancient world. We are dealing here with a mindset that underlies much of the legal debate between Jesus and the Jewish authorities as depicted in the Synoptic Gospels (see Mt 23:25–26; Mk 7:1–23; Lk 7:36–50), and is a major factor in the practical application of Paul's theology of freedom from the Law. Yet it is a set of categories extremely difficult for the modern Westerner to understand, a mindset which we encounter today practically nowhere except in orthodox Judaism which continues it as part of the living legacy of the Mosaic Law.

Rules of clean and unclean have to do with harmony and purity, with what fits and does not fit according to a perceived cosmic order. They set procedures for order in society and boundaries of behavior. They are concerned with preserving these appropriate boundaries of the social body as well as the individual body. Infraction of the rules is violation of order, and is to be carefully distinguished from moral guilt. The unclean is that which does not belong: dirt, disorder, rudeness.

These rules also set off the realms of sacred and profane, the divine and the human, from one another—a separation much more acute in ancient thinking than in ours. The categories of sacred and profane are worked out in all religions in terms of time, space, and conduct. Thus some days are meant for a special purpose, be they sabbath, Sunday, or Memorial Day. Some places are reserved for special purposes, be they temple, chapel, or the Tomb of the Unknown Soldier. Some behavior is appropriate in some times and places and others not. Modern American society suffers from an impoverishment of these instincts of holy and ordinary, even of proper and improper. Other than the minimal rituals with which we surround sexual and excretory functions (and current debates about pornography even throw these in doubt), there are very few such observances in our lives.

Malina points out that Jesus' apparent heedlessness of the purity rules of his culture (touching lepers, healing on the sabbath, etc.), when put in the context of his debates with religious authorities, was not violation of rules but the prophetic attempt to put detailed rules within the broader context of God's sovereignty over all. The first Christian generation followed his lead by adapting the notions of holy and ordinary, clean and unclean, to their changed circumstances without a Temple cult, a holy people in the midst of the world.

Conclusion

This partial summary of the treatment of "first century consciousness" from B. Malina's *The New Testament World: Insights from Cultural Anthropology* is meant to be an invitation to read the book itself, an excellently readable introduction to the world and mentality of those who lived and wrote the New Testament. My regrets are only two: that so many of the modern examples are heavily collegiate since the book is valuable for a much wider audience, and that there are not more first century non-biblical sources drawn upon rather than in some cases large numbers of Old Testament examples from centuries earlier. We will have occasion to draw upon these categories, especially those of honor and shame, individual and group, and marriage and family in the discussions that follow.

Part II
SLAVE AND FREE:
ECONOMIC AND SOCIAL
STATUS

3
The Jesus Movement

In the preceding pages we have sketched the historical, cultural, and social background of Palestine in the years that were formative for the setting of Jesus' ministry. Now it is time to turn our attention to the people who were caught up in that movement. Who were they? From what backgrounds? What motivated them and what were the social patterns within the movement itself in the first years? How did Jesus and his followers relate to the economic and social structures of their world? These are some of the questions that have been asked by recent writers who have attempted to observe the Jesus movement through the lens of social science models.

Galilean Society

Since the first followers of Jesus were nearly all Galileans, it will be helpful to look briefly at the social stratification of Galilee at the time as outlined by Freyne.[1] At the base of the economic and social system were the peasants (Malina's "villagers") with their ancestral and largely unchanging rural way of life, whether as owners of their own land or as tenant farmers, perhaps transformed from former to latter by temporary agricultural disaster from which they never recovered their independence. They were largely uninvolved in the wider commercial activity and thus less influenced by Hellenism than other groups. Their focus was village life with its closed patterns of kinship and loyalty that could remain relatively unchanged while empires came and went.

Closely related to the peasant class were the "rural proletariat"—the rootless day laborers, itinerant craftsmen, and brigands of the countryside and villages. These were people with their origins and sympathies in the peasant way of life, but with less stability in their lives and therefore more unrest brought on by a deeper awareness of economic and social disparity (consider the day laborers of Matthew 20:1–16 who are at the mercy of a vineyard owner's whim). Because of their situation of subsistence living without access to the land with all its symbolic as well as economic significance, they had less to lose than the land-bound peasants by looking for alternatives to their present existence.

A third level of Galilean society was constituted by the class of lesser officials which grew up in the Hellenistic system, perhaps originally belonging to the Greek civil occupationary group, but by the time of Jesus nearly all Jewish: local judges and civil administrators, lesser tax collectors, stewards of absentee landlords, most with no great love for their social inferiors (compare the hostility of tenants for stewards and landlords in Mark 12:2–8 with the steward's manipulation of tenants in Luke 16:1–8).

At the top of the Galilean stratification were the Jewish aristocracy of the cities (Malina's "urban elite"), who owed their status to the Hellenistic urbanization of Palestine. Residents of urban centers like Sepphoris or Tiberias, they often owned vast estates that had been previously confiscated from the peasants and tax farming concessions whose control depended on the pleasure of the ruling authorities. Many of the provincial aristocracy owed their rise to Herod the Great's distribution of land to his supporters some fifty years before; their status maintenance depended on their continued support of Herodian and Roman interests. Thus they were seen by the rest of the population as supporters of the foreign occupation. The "Herodians" of the Gospels (Mark 3:6; 12:13) may have belonged to this group.

When trying to establish clearly defined social classes in any society, we must remember that the actual situation was more complex than anything that can be neatly classified, and that from such a distance in time it is extremely difficult to construct societal patterns which were much more a matter of everyday unspoken experience than literary record. Nevertheless, some general lines do emerge, and these can be spoken of as we do here. An important thing to remember is that in the Mediterranean world status depended far less on income and lifestyle than on birth and inherited situation. In contemporary American society social class is an illusive reality with fluid boundaries that are easily crossed by changes in income, job status, education, and change of location. Whatever the reality, the democratic ideal holds that all are citizens with identical rights and that the possibility of social and economic betterment is open to all. Though we shall later see that there were some exceptions, generally Greco-Roman society was quite different. Privilege, wealth, and full civil rights belonged only to those born into a certain status, who passed it on to the next generation. Those without it could give their progeny only more of the inferior status that had been theirs for generations.

Early Christianity as Millenarianism

With these social factors as backdrop, many have tried to understand just what was the appeal of Jesus' preaching to those who first followed him and how his quick popularity is explainable in terms of what we know of the life of those first followers. One of the first writers of the new social science approach to tackle these questions was John Gager in *Kingdom and Community: The Social World of Early Christianity*. Drawing upon the research of cultural anthropologists regarding other known millenarian movements,[2] Gager attempts in his second chapter to understand the dynamics of Jesus' ministry and the early years of the Church as a movement of dramatic expectation.

The term "Millenarianism" as used here bears no necessary relation to the idea of Christ's thousand-year reign on earth as narrated in Revelation 20:1–7. Rather it refers to the expectation of "a new order of reality in the near future,"[3] a reversal of the present order in which wrongs will be righted. Such movements are usually characterized by a quick burst of enthusiasm and short life span, often centered around a charismatic, prophetic leader who is not necessarily the cause of the movement but serves to focus its energy and embody its new vision in himself/herself.

Because of the belief in the imminent reversal of the social order, the group usually begins to live out this vision in initial ways: social and/or sexual egalitarianism and the minimizing of social structures. There is a strong sense of boundaries, of who belongs and who doesn't, and these norms of membership and status tend to reverse those of the larger society, over against which the millenarian group sees itself: those who think themselves in the "in" group are really "out of it," and vice versa (see Mk 10:31; Mt 20:16; Lk 13:30: "The first shall be last and the last first," the same saying in three entirely different contexts).

To whom would such a movement most appeal? Much but not all research indicates of course the disinherited, the disadvantaged of society, who have the most to gain by having the tables turned. Characteristically, money and its related activities are seen as sources of corruption and perverted symbols of human worth, whereas the new order will provide heavenly compensation for poverty and restore the proper criteria for human dignity (see Mt 5:3; Lk 6:20–26; Mk 10:21–23; Jas 2:5; 5:1–6). If the appeal is not always to those at the very bottom of the social scale, it is at least to those who experience "relative deprivation," the frustration of unfulfilled hopes and the insecurity of an uncertain future. The hopelessness of the unenlightened oppressed may actually constitute a security that is harder to shake loose, whereas those who are aware of their plight and have had their hopes stirred up are a dangerously volatile force.

As must be obvious by now, the model of millenarian groups is a helpful perspective from which to approach the first years of the Jesus movement. Other apocalyptic preachers are known to have surfaced in Palestine in the years prior to Jesus' ministry, and many of the later Old Testament books (Ezekiel, Daniel, Second and Third Isaiah, etc.) hold out the promise of just such a reversal of the social order, where peace and prosperity will be open to all under the reign of God. Jesus' insistence on the transcendent element of the Kingdom which is nevertheless here and now (Mk 1:14; Mt 12:28; 19:14; Lk 13:28–29) did not prevent even his closest disciples from thinking that a political revolution was in the offing (Acts 1:6). The strong call to justice, integrity, and peace would have appealed most strongly precisely to those most conscious that they were being deprived of it: the peasants and village craftspersons (the group from which Jesus himself came), the marginalized and the dispossessed.

In saying this, however, we must beware of being overly simplistic or romantic. Many such people were not at all poverty-stricken: Zebedee had hired laborers (Mk 1:20) and skilled artisans held a certain status in village society. Moreover, one of the disciples was a tax collector, and Jesus attracted the favorable attention of a synagogue official (Mk 5:22), a Pharisee (Lk 7:36), a rich member of a town council (Mt 27:57; Lk 23:50–51), even a Roman military officer (Lk 7:2–10). One of the remarkable characteristics of Jesus' ministry is his ability to move in and out of various status groups: peasants, townspeople, tax collectors and prostitutes (who, though they are lumped together in Matthew 21:31–32, would by no means have identified with each other), Pharisees and well-to-do urbanites. The key to social class in the Mediterranean world was not income but *status.* Usually but not always, wealth or lack of it was proportionate to status.

With that qualification raised, still it can be said that there are great similarities between what we know of the origins of the Jesus movement and other millenarian movements. Those people in the most vulnerable positions in society were the most ready to hear the apocalyptic message of hope that the evil ways of the present system could soon be reversed in a gigantic sweeping action of God's just hand.

Cognitive Dissonance

It has long been a question among scholars of early Christianity how the expectation of an imminent and cataclysmic end of the present order was transformed into an historical faith. Whatever was Jesus' intention, it can hardly be doubted that the oral tradition about him and the New Testament writings contain definite elements of such an expectation (see for instance Mk 9:1; 13:30; 1 Thes 4:15–17). What happened when the Parousia, the final coming of Christ, was delayed? The apocalyptic message had to be reinterpreted and accommodated to a way of life that intended to continue indefinitely in history: imminent expectation became continual watchfulness, the apocalyptic symbols became ways of interpreting history.

In the second section of chapter 2 of *Kingdom and Community,* Gager draws on another social science theory to interpret the early Christian response to the delay of the Parousia: cognitive dissonance.[4] This theory, based on the study of many apocalyptic-prophetic groups, postulates that when a group's fundamental religious beliefs are disconfirmed, one possible result is dissolution, but this is not the only possibility. Instead, the group may intensify its fervor and translate this energy into an expanded missionary movement. The greater the dissonance between expectation and result, the greater the need to reassess, reinterpret, and convert others.

Thus the disciples' expectation that Jesus during his life would establish the earthly Kingdom of God was disconfirmed in the totally disconcerting event of his crucifixion. Even though the Gospels portray Jesus as having predicted it during his lifetime (Mk 8:31–33; 9:31–32; 10:33–34, with parallels in Matthew and Luke), the consistent reaction of the disciples is disbelief and lack of comprehension, even after they have heard reports of his having been raised (Lk 24:21–24). Indeed they seem to have been, understandably, more bewildered by this than by his death. Soon they came to the realization that the resurrection was partly confirming of their expectations, yet it intensified expectation of the final coming, for which it was seen as an imminent preparation.

The delay of the Parousia became a second element of disconfirmation, however. This is reflected as a problem in such texts as 2 Peter 3:3–10 and James 5:7–9 with their message of patient hope for the coming of the Lord who is nevertheless on the way despite an apparent slowdown in the projected time frame. Again, disconfirmation seems to evoke a renewal of fervor, a reassessment and recommitment to a firm belief and way of life and vigorous attempts to convert others. The support of group reinforcement is crucial for continued survival and vitality of belief; of this element there is no lack of evidence in the strong community structure of early Christianity as we see it manifested especially in Acts and the Pauline epistles.

The confusion caused by disconfirmation of the expectation brings two different kinds of response in a group that survives the crisis: the intellectual response of reassessment and reinterpretation (we misunderstood; the timing was wrong; patient waiting is more important than realization), and the social response of proselytism or mission activity (the compulsion to carry forth the word and expand the number of believers). Both elements can clearly be seen operating in the first years of Christianity, and Gager has alerted us to an important new perspective from which to examine the New Testament events.

The weakest point in the application of cognitive dissonance theory to early Christianity is in my opinion the function of the resurrection which, as much as it seems to have taken the disciples by surprise, can only be seen within the scope of the theory as a strongly *confirming* faith event which generated energy to almost totally eclipse the disconfirmation of Jesus' death among believers and the delay of his final coming as well, enabling the reinterpretation of the Parousia to be made with more ease. Admittedly the "scandal of the cross" in missionary efforts among believers remained a serious obstacle (1 Cor 1:20–25). But cognitive dissonance theory and Gager's analysis are concerned primarily with the inner dynamics of the group of believers.

The final section of chapter 2 of *Kingdom and Community* deals with the Book of Revelation as exemplar of the way in which apocalyptic vision can be a means of sublimated attainment of millennial bliss through a sort of therapeutic purification. Though the social function of apocalyptic literature is an object of much current interest, the treatment in this section is done within a more psychoanalytic framework, which takes us outside the scope of the present investigation. Those interested in the psychic structure of symbolic function will find it helpful.

Wandering Charismatics

Another recent writer who has attempted to apply social science models to what we know of the early Jesus movement is Gerd Theissen, whose work first appeared in German in 1977 as a "sociology of the Jesus movement," with English translation the next year entitled more generally *Sociology of Early Palestinian Christianity*.[5] His procedure is to investigate roles, other social factors, and functions of early Christianity in its original environment under three aspects: constructive conclusions assembling data, analytic conclusions regarding function, and comparative conclusions relating these factors to other possibly related situations in the Greco-Roman world.

Examining the evidence of the Gospels, Theissen proposes that Jesus did not establish communities, but groups of itinerants with a lifestyle characterized by renouncement of home, family, possessions, and protection, a lifestyle quite similar to that of itinerant Cynic philosophers in the Greek world and possibly influenced by it. These "wandering charismatics" were the core of Jesus' followers, materially supported wherever they went by "local sympathizers" grouped in communities. These resident sympathizers were less radical in their lifestyle than the itinerants, and their ethos depended largely on the principles of behavior and procedure enunciated in the Gospels.

The focus of both groups was of course Jesus himself, the "bearer of revelation," whose proclamation of the imminent Kingdom gave meaning to the counter-societal aspects of this Jewish reform movement. As Son of Man suffering (Mk 8:31; 9:31; 10:33–34) and soon to be glorified (Mk 8:38; 13:26; Mt 19:28), his identity and destiny bore enormously on their own, for their fate was the same: his suffering is mirrored in theirs, his glorification is the promise of theirs. Christology explains life.

Theissen goes on to examine the socio-economic, political, and cultural situation with the method given above, concluding that the "social rootlessness" which Jesus' wandering disciples exemplified (but which was not limited to them) was related to socio-economic factors of ambiguity and survival situations for some peasants and villagers in Palestine at this time. The tensions between rural and urban, upper and lower classes, wealthy and poor, foreign and indigenous, were deepening. Those with least to lose by abandoning social roots were the already dispossessed or squeezed out, of whatever class: peasants, a "marginal middle class" caught in-between, those who have known a better and more honorable way of living and have lost it. It is they who are most sensitive to suffering and deprivation, who yearn for deliverance of one kind or another, whereas those comfortably secure in whatever position are less acquainted with their own need for redemption. Jesus was a rural leader who avoided the great urban centers except the unavoidable Jerusalem.

The observant readers will note that much of the preceding paragraph sounds familiar. Theissen's socio-economic analyses in this book and other writings were a partial influence on Freyne's *Galilee*. Freyne has more carefully documented the literary, historical, archeological, and inscriptional evidence, tried some of Theissen's analyses, and found them to fit.

In regard to the political significance of the Jesus movement, Theissen characterizes it as a reform intended to purify and radicalize an already theoretically existing theocracy. The political crisis of the era for Judaism was the possibility of reviving the theocratic vision after a recent parade of foreign and less than successful native rulers.

The Jesus movement differed from most of the radical theocratic reform movements because, rather than incorporate anti-foreign sentiment as an essential ingredient, it preached a sometimes cautious yet persistent universalism—a factor which was ultimately to contribute to its downfall in Palestine and success in the Diaspora.

It is a sociological principle that one reaction to crisis is an intensification of norms, a renewal movement which will call members to a deepened commitment to the group and its original qualities. In the face of invasion by Hellenistic culture, most Jewish reform movements stressed more intense dedication to traditional cultural and religious values: the Law (Pharisees), the Temple (Sadducees), exclusivist notions of priesthood (Essenes). While some traditions about Jesus' preaching stressed respect for these traditions (e.g., Mt 5:17–19), others challenged them with universalist claims that transcended Jewish ethnocentrism (e.g., Mk 7:14–19; Mt 28:19–20), picked up the universalist trends of post-exilic prophecy, and laid the foundations for a missionary movement that could thrive in the cosmopolitan pluralistic environment of the Roman world.

Theissen has been criticized for an absence of carefully laid theoretical foundation and consequent lack of explicit articulation of his theoretical framework, which is largely that of structural functionalism. Like Gager, he also dips occasionally into psychoanalytic models, a far more questionable procedure given the dearth of individualized data and the vast differences in consciousness described in Malina's *New Testament World* discussed in Chapter 2 above. Theissen also has a tendency to maintain too sharply the distinction between "Palestinian" and "Hellenistic" Judaism, despite his knowledge and use of Hengel's *Judaism and Hellenism*. Nevertheless his critical analyses have proved to be helpful contributions toward a better understanding of the social dynamics behind the New Testament.

Human and Divine at Work

The readers will recall that in Chapter 1 I spoke of the potential danger in this social science approach of reducing the spiritual dynamic of the Bible to a purely social one. At the same time I cautioned about the opposite danger of ignoring the realistic human factors in the formation of the Bible and thus missing an important part of the splendor of our Christian heritage. The above discussions of the work of Gager and Theissen could give the impression of swinging too far in the first direction by presenting the Gospels as reflections of only social, political, and economic factors. But both Gager and Theissen acknowledge that there are far more than these at work in the development of the New Testament and the effect of Jesus on history. The transcendent divine action here is taken for granted because to cover it is not the scope of this book or of any book on which I am reporting. This is not theology strictly speaking but preparation for it and implementation of the theological principle that God usually communicates to us through ordinary human instruments.

4
Paul and the People of His World

Several years ago a TV special[1] followed the missionary careers of Peter and Paul as they moved out of the Palestinian context into the larger world of the Roman Empire in its finest years. After a good many years of more or less successful evangelizing in the quieter towns of Asia Minor, Cyprus, and Macedonia, Paul began to set his sights on the intellectual center of Athens. He was warned by his friends that the sophisticated citizens of the "big city" would not be as receptive to his philosophically unpalatable message as had been the less sophisticated people with whom he had been dealing in more backward areas.

The enthusiastic Paul ignored the warning, marched into Athens, and proceeded to address the intellectual types gathered on the Areopagus—somewhat equivalent to giving a public lecture in a university town—with the speech attributed to him in Acts 17. Sure enough, the warning came true. In spite of the clever beginning in which he claimed to know the unknown god whom they worshiped without knowing, at the mention of the resurrection of Jesus he was met by laughter and mockery. The notion of bodily resurrection was rejected as naive wishful thinking from some backwater place like Palestine.

Though any modern depiction of New Testament events includes some exaggeration for the sake of effect, there is an element of truth in the way the story is told. Paul was a man of the Greco-Roman world, a native Greek speaker, a Hellenistic Jew. His Greek background was of inestimable value to him in his work in the Diaspora mission. Yet his rabbinic education brought him into direct contact with the literary and theological sources of his faith and ethnic culture. As a Pharisee he represented one of the most prominent and progressive groups in the Palestinian Judaism of his day. Paul's challenge was to translate faith in Jesus from a rural peasant language to that of a sophisticated urban culture. In the process, like any creative and visionary thinker, he made many friends and many enemies.

The Cosmopolitan World of the Christian Mission

The Roman world of Paul's day was a civilization that had never been surpassed for the grandeur of its undertakings. The artistic and intellectual inheritance of Greece, from which the Romans never begged but freely borrowed and stole, was combined with Roman superiority in technology and political organization to produce a way of life that unified the Mediterranean world from one end to the other in a common urban civilization.

Like any civilization, it had its systems of social stratification whose subtleties are somewhat elusive to us who are separated from it by time and distance. Nevertheless a great deal can be known about the social system of the Roman imperial period, the time of the writing of the New Testament. It was a system that worked horizontally and vertically in different ways from a modern Western culture, where social status depends mostly on economic level and affordable lifestyle, where the nuclear family is the norm, and where the democratic ideal precludes formal stratification of society into a hierarchy of superiors and inferiors.

The ancient world, on the other hand, did not associate economic level and social status as closely as we do. Rather, the status into which one was born was usually accompanied by a corresponding economic level, but with rare exceptions it was the family and legal status to which one belonged that mattered far more than financial affluence or lack of it. The hierarchical extended family concept at every level of society created a coherent pattern of social structure with clear positions of superiority and subordination (this will be further developed in chapter 6 when we examine the intent of the household codes in the later books of the New Testament).

The Roman social order[2] was topped by two groups or *ordines* of aristocrats—first, the senatorial *ordo* whose members were eligible for the highest civil and religious posts; second, the lesser aristocratic *ordo* of the equestrians or knights who formed the backbone of second-rung administrators in the Empire. Pontius Pilate, Felix and Festus (Acts 23–25), successive prefects of Judea, were probably equestrians, answerable to a senatorial-rank governor in Syria like the earlier Quirinius (see Lk 2:2). As these two aristocratic *ordines* became decimated by civil wars and political purges, their ranks were filled by members of the aristocratic families from the occupied provinces, who naturally brought with them not only their ethnic and cultural differences, but diverse worldviews as well. The aristocratic Roman sentiments of nobility, virtue, and conservatism idealized by the old senatorial families slowly gave way to the sophisticated cosmopolitan outlook of the newer set out to make their own way in the world and serve Rome at the same time.

Below the ranks of aristocrats were the freeborn lower classes, about whom we know least of all, perhaps because their lot changed the least from generation to generation. The quiet backbone of the free labor force, they went about their lives without leaving much of an effect on either the literary or archeological evidence that has survived. In Rome at least there were regular distributions of free grain for them out of the imperial treasury, and in all major urban centers public banquets, celebrations, and entertainment were provided chiefly with them in mind by both public and private beneficence.

In the hierarchical social structure as it is being described here, those at the bottom are the slaves and freedmen/women. Whether born into slavery or enslaved as war captives, kidnap victims, or convicted criminals, slaves had no legal rights and were theoretically legal non-persons. On the agricultural estates and in the mines theirs was an unenviable fate. Urban slavery was somewhat different, however. Household slaves often had a great deal of independence and responsibility. Those with good education were teachers. Much of the effective administration of the imperial household with its vast international network was in the hands of slaves and freedmen. Statistical studies of the inscriptional and literary evidence of the period show that a high number of slaves received their freedom ("manumission") in midlife.

Many of these people became successful in business or civil service, advanced socially as well as economically, and became rich and powerful. It was not unusual for a family over the span of two or three generations to go from slavery to a fairly well-to-do economic and social level, and eventually perhaps even to gain access to the equestrian *ordo* and beyond. The second century freedman philosopher Epictetus lamented that slaves dream only about emancipation, then making money, entering the equestrian *ordo,* gaining a military command and eventually access to the senate, where they would find themselves more enslaved by their situation than when they were actually slaves.[3] The comment is to be taken as social commentary as well as philosophical satire.

If the freedmen/women class had the least to lose, they had the most to gain. As "nouveaux riches" they could be ostentatious and overbearing with their wealth. The literature of the period is punctuated with the resentful comments of aristocrats who consider their displays of pomp tasteless. This is not to assume that every emancipated slave became wealthy, but a good number apparently did, enough to give the whole group the reputation for being socially and commercially aggressive. The goal for which they yearned was the cultured and leisured life of the landed aristocracy.

No matter how hard they worked or how wealthy they became however, freedmen were still excluded from full acceptance into that ruling group and from the most prestigious political appointments and positions (though their descendants might gain access to them). This difference, made officially by social stratification and reinforced unofficially by discrimination, marks the distinction between *ordo* as juridically and hierarchically understood, and social class as a more fluid indicator of one's power based on wealth and influence. Both factors operated in the New Testament world as conditions affecting what one could or could not do. Paul's famous comment in 1 Corinthians 1:27 probably refers to both systems: not many of the Corinthian Christians, he says, were sophisticated or powerful (probably indicators of education, culture, wealth, and influence) or well born (definitely an indicator of hierarchical social status by family). The examples of women are also illustrative: though women are known throughout Roman times to have participated in business and trade guilds and to have exercised considerable influence through wealth and social position, no woman is ever known to have held a major political or administrative appointment (precisely those positions reserved for the hierarchically elite group), and the structural position of women in Roman society always remained inferior to that of men.

There are of course many other characteristics of the Roman urban world which affected the New Testament. Several more can be briefly singled out as significant: the patron-client relationship, various types of social organizations, and the function of mobility.[4]

Because of the different types of social stratification described above, people in the Roman world did not generally assume that "all are created equal," or at least that equality was given in social relations. Rather, the ranking of some as superior and others as inferior on the basis of birth, family, or position led to an elaborate structuring of relationships between social unequals on the basis of a patronage system that greatly enhanced the smooth operation of society. The beneficent and generous protection of the great was expected in return for the gratitude, adulation, and faithful service of the dependent. Thus one of the best ways to gain social advancement and preference was to ingratiate oneself with a powerful person from whose generosity one hoped to benefit. The system extended from the private to the public level. Even kings owed their position to those more powerful, as clients of their patron: the relation of the Herodian rulers in Palestine to the Roman emperor is a good example. Public works for the benefit of citizens were often financed by wealthy patrons, thus placing a whole populace in the position of client. In such a society, intricate patterns of dependence develop and overlap, creating a fabric of loyalties that is an important part of the social structure.

If the patron-client system fostered unequal relationships, the system of social clubs or organizations encouraged the interchange of equals. Some were predominantly religious organizations, formed around the cult of a certain deity, others were formed on the basis of a common trade or occupation, still others were burial societies, whose principal purpose seems to have been the collection of funds to ensure a suitable and dignified burial of the members. Such organizations, usually called *collegia* in Latin or *thiasoi* in Greek, were not unidimensional, however, for the characteristics of all three of these types could be, and frequently were, combined in one grouping. The club may sometimes have been sustained by a wealthy patron or patroness, but members could be freeborn or freed, even slaves in some cases, usually male but also on occasion female. The associations had membership dues, entrance fees, a constitution, and officers with important-sounding titles. Though often organized on the basis of common occupations, they did not function like medieval trade guilds or modern labor unions but seem to have been mostly social in nature.

It was suggested long ago that this kind of organization may have been the basic model for the urban Christian communities, for whom common cult was certainly the major element, and whom we know at least from the end of the second century to have taken it upon themselves to provide for the burial of members. It is now generally accepted that whatever the similarities between the two types of groups, there are sufficient dissimilarities that Christian communities would probably not have been seen as just another kind of *thiasos* among many.

Because of the excellent road system that was one of the benefits of Roman rule, the possibilities for mobility on the part of even non-royalty and non-military in the Roman world were unrivaled . The first century of the Christian era was a time of enormous commercial prosperity and exchange, when major trade centers like Antioch, Thessalonica, Corinth, and Rome saw people from the ends of the Mediterranean world pass through them plying their trades. The great urban centers were the places in which not only commerce but literary and intellectual discourse took place, fed by the steady stream of travelers who passed through and often stayed a while, philosophers and scholars as well as traders and business people. Because of this high degree of travel and mobility, new ideas as well as foreign goods could reach everywhere. The Christians in Paul's world who seem to be frequently on the move (besides Paul himself and his missionary companions), e.g. Prisca and Aquila (Acts 18:2, 18, etc.), Lydia the cloth merchant at Philippi (Acts 16:14), Phoebe of Cenchrae bound for Rome (Rom 16:1–2), and Apollos of Alexandria (Acts 18:24; 1 Cor 1:12), to name only a few, are probably not exceptions to a common pattern. They may in fact have taken advantage of business trips to do religious work as well—or vice versa.

Paul's Social Status

Having seen some of the factors which created the social and cultural environment in which Pauline Christianity flourished, let us now turn to Paul himself and attempt to situate him in that environment.

We know a number of things about Paul relevant to his social status. From Paul's own letters we know that he was a Jew and belonged to that religious party within Judaism known as the Pharisees. From his writing style we know that his Greek literary education was adequate, and that he was also well versed in the methods of biblical exegesis that he could only have learned by study with Jewish scholars. We know from 1 Corinthians 9 and elsewhere that on principle he refused to accept financial support from most of the communities he served, but insisted on earning his own sustenance by working at a manual skill even though the opposite was customary for apostles. An exception seems to have been Philippi in Macedonia, from whose Christians he accepted gifts (see Phil 4:14–18; 2 Cor 11:8–9).

From the Acts of the Apostles we learn other details about Paul's social standing which Paul himself does not mention, chiefly that he was a citizen of the city of Tarsus in southeastern Asia Minor and a Roman citizen as well. In addition, it is Acts which specifies that his trade was tentmaking, which perhaps means leather working in general. Because the author seems to have definite literary and theological purposes in the presentation of some material, the data from Acts must be used with caution. But, on the other hand, they are not to be ignored.

A recent book by Ronald Hock, *The Social Context of Paul's Ministry,* attempts to situate Paul in his social milieu by means of his trade. He points out first of all that the term given by Acts for Paul's trade, *skēnopoios,* can refer to any kind of working with tanned leather—stitching tents, making shoes, leather binding, etc. Paul gives evidence of having had a literary education that would have placed him in a different social grouping than that of leather craftsmen.[5] What is he doing in the workshop?

The traditional way of understanding this mixture of roles has been to attribute it to Paul's Jewish sub-culture and especially to his rabbinic training. Later rabbinic advice praises the combination of study of the Law with some other occupation. Hock questions this association, and suggests that instead we look to the wider Greco-Roman culture in which Paul participated. There we find the model of the Stoic-Cynic philosopher, the best known type of sage figure in his day. The philosophers were able to support themselves in one or more of four ways: charging fees for their instruction, attaching themselves as clients to wealthy patrons as "scholar in residence" in the household, begging (the most extreme alternative which only the hardiest chose), or working at some form of trade by which they could be self-employed, earning only as much as they needed for their bodily needs while still having time to devote to teaching and study. Some who chose this last alternative even carried on philosophical discourse in the setting of the workshop, a tradition that goes back at least as far as Socrates.

To understand this association with Paul, we must recall that a "philosophy" in the Hellenistic world is not merely an intellectual system debated by scholars. It is rather a way of living wisely which is proposed by its teachers to whoever can grasp it in order to know the way of truth and live accordingly. Sometimes followers of a particular philosopher lived together in a communal ascetic lifestyle. With this in mind, one can see how early Christian communities were often seen as "philosophies" and hence its teachers as "philosophers."

In a previous article[6] Hock had developed the argument that not only what we know of Paul's education, but even his terminology and attitudes toward work classify him as one from "the socially privileged classes" who has voluntarily taken on a trade which otherwise would be socially beneath him. Here Hock goes on to argue that the principal reason for Paul's insistence on earning his own way is his wish to identify with the most dignified way of life of the philosopher, with one who is neither mercenary in charging fees nor servile in being dependent on a wealthy patron. Paul's insistence on his freedom in 1 Corinthians 9:1, 19 would echo this sentiment.

Apparently the Corinthian Christians were not pleased by this stand on Paul's part (see 1 Cor 9; 2 Cor 11:7–11; 12:13–16). This may have been because they thought such manual labor was demeaning for their apostle, whereas the "super apostles" against whom Paul contends in 2 Corinthians 11 and 12 either followed the usual custom of accepting hospitality from the communities, or had more dignified means of livelihood. Another reason, of course, may have been that Paul was thus more independent and less answerable to them. Still a third possible reason, suggested by G. Theissen (whose book on Pauline Christianity will be discussed below), is that the "command of the Lord" cited by Paul in 1 Corinthians 9:14 about missionaries getting their living from the Gospel was intended not so much to authoritatively compel communities to support their missionaries as it was to compel missionaries to live in voluntary poverty, dependent upon the generosity of others. According to this explanation, Paul balks at taking this radical stand for his own reasons, and the Corinthians are attempting to recall him to his responsibility as they see it.

Whatever the reason for Paul's insistence on economic independence from most of his communities, his position echoes the ideal of simplicity and independence proposed particularly by the Stoic philosophers, but also represented in the Jewish wisdom tradition. This notion of *autarkeia,* or "self-sufficiency," later became a strong theme in Christian monasticism. It represents a middle ground between radical asceticism on the one hand and enslavement to one's passions and desires on the other. By being independent of human means and therefore of social pressures, as well as remaining indifferent to the needs and wants of the appetites, the person who is *autarkēs* could be truly free, inwardly and outwardly. Paul's strongest expressions of this ideal for himself are his warning against enslavement to passion in 1 Corinthians 6:12 and his remarks about being content whether in abundance or want in Philippians 4:11–13.[7] Such attitudes are most likely to come from one who has had the education, leisure, and prosperity to know both sides of the situation and critically reflect on his experience.

Class, Status, and Conflict at Corinth

Having seen what we can surmise about Paul's social status, let us now turn to the investigation of the status of the first generation of Christians in the cities of the Roman world. At the beginning of this century came discoveries of many written documents from the ordinary life of people in the same era as that of the New Testament. These thousands of legal contracts, personal letters, dinner invitations, elementary school exercises, etc. were preserved on papyrus in the hot dry climate of Egypt. These discoveries revolutionized the study of biblical Greek by making scholars aware that the language of the New Testament was much closer to the ordinary spoken Greek of the day than they had thought. These discoveries seemed to confirm the accusation of the second century pagan philosopher Celsus that Christians came from and addressed themselves to only the lowest classes in soci-

ety, the ignorant, the poor, the credulous. The language of these everyday documents suggested to the great scholar of papyrology, G.A.
Deissmann, that the New Testament was written by and for members
of the middle and lower classes, since much of it reflected the same
style, devoid of the better classicist literary style known from the more
sophisticated literature of the same period.[8]

Since Deissmann, however, others have questioned these conclusions, notably the Australian classicist, E.A. Judge, who suggested in
a little book published in 1960 that the evidence both of the New Testament itself and of social patterns in its environment indicates much
more of a social mix, and particularly the influence of persons of
higher social status and prosperity who would have been looked to for
leadership and financial support after the pattern of the patron-client
relationship.[9] Since then there has been somewhat of a growing con-
sensus that Christianity as it moved into the urban society of the
Roman world was not so much a popular movement of the poor and
dispossessed (the "proletariat" of earlier Marxist interpreters) as it
was a truly cross-sectional representation of Greco-Roman society,
with the possible omission of the highest *ordines* and the lowest
"dregs."

Recently there have appeared two major studies on the social status of the first Christian generation in the Roman world: Gerd Theissen's *The Social Setting of Pauline Christianity: Essays on Corinth,*[10]
and Wayne Meeks' *The First Urban Christians: The Social World of
the Apostle Paul.* What is said of Theissen could be said as well of
Meeks, that "It would seem fair to characterize his interests as more
those of the social historian than those of the sociologist."[11] Thus for
Meeks the double task of the social historian, which he sets for himself, is to "try to discern the textures of life in particular times and
particular places" and "to describe the life of the ordinary Christian
within that environment."[12] For both authors theory is helpful only
insofar as it can illuminate the historical and social situation of early
Christianity. Neither seems interested in the further step of verifica-
tion of a theory per se for its possible use in other cultural settings, as
would be the social scientist. Thus Theissen and Meeks are rather typical of the biblical scholars and historians of early Christianity who
have entered the field of social study of ancient texts: their focus and

primary interest remains the world of early Christianity rather than a cross-cultural application of social science models.

Because of the length and nature of Paul's two letters to Corinth,[13] we have more information about that community than about any other in Paul's world. Both books therefore deal with the Pauline communities in general, but ultimately come to rest on the Corinthian correspondence.

Using as a starting point the theme of the "wandering charismatic" which is developed further in his *Sociology of Early Palestinian Christianity,* Theissen's first chapter develops the supposed difference between that form of missionary activity and another which he calls "community organizer." Here the issue is legitimation, focused on the question of community support for the missionary. Theissen distinguishes three types of basis for establishing the legitimacy of one's claims to missionary authority and acceptance: charismatic legitimation based on a certain lifestyle recognized as appropriately ascetic; traditional legitimation based on origins of teaching and authorization; functional legitimation based on observable achievements.

He suggests that the problem of Paul's self-support, raised especially in 1 Corinthians 9, has to do with the favorable impression left on the Corinthians by other "charismatic" missionaries whose voluntary poverty and dependence on community generosity seem among other factors to legitimate them in the eyes of the local Christians. In addition, they can appeal to the best source, probably the Jerusalem church, for their authorization: they seem not only holy but in possession of impeccable credentials as well. By contrast Paul insists that the missionary's support from the community is a right, not an obligation. He appeals rather to the effects of his ministry among them (functional), to his authorization by the risen Christ himself (traditional), and to his own type of charismatic heroics, the preaching of the cross and the absurdity of weakness (1 Cor 1). Thus Theissen argues that the question of the apostle's material subsistence and the question of his theological legitimacy are tightly bound to each other.

Both Theissen and Meeks give a great deal of attention to the question of social stratification within the Pauline communities. Theissen's second chapter focuses on the information that can be gleaned about Corinthian Christians. On the basis of the evidence available,

Theissen argues that while most of the community come from "the lower classes," by contrast there are some members from "the upper classes," mostly those who are sufficiently influential to have their names mentioned.

Theissen's exegesis of 1 Corinthians 1:26–29 proposes that while most of the Corinthian community are socially inconsequential, on the contrary some are capable of being singled out because of position by birth or status. Examples include Crispus of 1 Corinthians 1:14 who according to Acts 18:8 is an *archisynagōgos* or synagogue official; Stephanas of 1 Corinthians 1:16 whose "household" identifies him as well-to-do; Gaius of 1 Corinthians 1:14, also baptized by Paul, and suggested in Romans 16:23 as having a house large enough to host not only Paul but the whole community for its assembly; Prisca and Aquila, Paul's great merchant friends, who also host a house church in Romans 16:5; and especially Erastus, the city treasurer of Romans 16:23, who may be identified with the *aedile* (superintendent of public works) named in an inscription of approximately the same period still preserved near the theatre of Corinth.

In addition, Pauline Christians engage in an extraordinary amount of travel over and above what we know to be direct missionary work: Prisca (Priscilla) and Aquila are connected with at least three different cities; Phoebe in Romans 16:1–2 seems about to undertake a journey with Paul's letter from Corinth to Rome; Chloe's people (1 Cor 1:11) have caught up with Paul elsewhere; Stephanas has arrived from Corinth to Ephesus with Fortunatus and Achaichus, possibly his slaves or freedmen, before the completion of 1 Corinthians (1 Cor 16:17), etc. Some of this travel may have been for the express purpose of delivering messages and letters to or from Paul, but more probably these are people moving about for their own business or personal reasons, from whose travel the churches profit to communicate with one another. When the information we have from Acts and the Pauline letters is laid out alongside what we know of the social and economic patterns of the cities in which these people lived, the conclusion which emerges is that the dominant evidence is in favor of rather high prosperity and social status for the Christians whose names we know. This of course says nothing about the silent majority.

Theissen carries this information in the direction of portraying the Corinthian community as test case for what may have been true in every early Christian community: that the social stratification of society in general carried over into the experience of Christians and came into conflict with the Christian ideal of fundamental equality before God. In other words, the Corinthian Christians, like Christians of any age, did not cease being affected by the variant values of their world all the while that they could proclaim the abolition of differences between Jew and Greek, slave and free, male and female in Christ (Gal 3:28, 1 Cor 12:13; Col 3:11).

The third and fourth chapters of *The Social Setting of Pauline Christianity* apply this assumption to the theological debates joined by Paul in 1 Corinthians 8, 10, and 11 about the question of meat sacrificed to idols and social discrimination at the Lord's Supper. In 1 Corinthians 8 and 10 the issue is whether a Christian can: buy meat freely in the marketplace even though it may be surplus from the morning sacrifice in a nearby pagan temple; accept an invitation to dinner in a temple dining room rented for the occasion where such meat will certainly be served, and where the meal will probably begin or end with a sacrifice to the god; accept an invitation to dinner at the home of a pagan who may be serving meat that came from a temple sacrifice.

"The strong" seem to have had no problem with these cases, arguing with a certain philosophical sophistication that since idols are not real gods anyway, the whole question is irrelevant. "The weak" were not so easily convinced, but rather got caught up in cases of conscience and were scandalized when they saw "the strong" blithely munching on sacrificed meat with the rationalization that "everything is permitted" (1 Cor 8:4–8; 10:23–29). Paul's solution places priority on the integrity of the community: scandal to another believer is to be avoided (1 Cor 8:9–13; 10:25–29; see also Rom 14), and if there is any question of seeming to participate in idol worship, it cannot be allowed (1 Cor 10:14–22). Otherwise do what you think best.

That much is clear from the text. It has generally been assumed, however, that the difference of opinion between the strong and weak is purely a theological one, between persons with different approaches of conscience, or between Jewish and Gentile Christians. By contrast what Theissen suggests is that there is a connection between these differences and social stratification. Only the wealthy would have meat on their table frequently enough to be used to it as a regular part of their diet and nothing special. Poorer people who would have it only on special occasions would be more likely to raise such questions. Moreover, the wealthy are more likely to have had the kind of education which would permit an intellectual analysis and solution to the problem. The poorer members of the community with less education would be more inclined to see it as an either/or situation.

Thus according to Theissen Paul is dealing here with theological and ethical differences of interpretation which are characteristic of different social classes. His opinion is that when there is no conflict resulting in potential scandal, indeed anything is permitted. When however such conflict arises, the strong (the upper class people) are to accommodate their behavior to the weak (the lower class). This solution is typical of Paul's love ethic which places preservation of the bond of unity above either social or theological purity.

In 1 Corinthians 11:17–22 another social problem appears. There are factions which split the community and turn the celebration of the Lord's Supper into a mockery. Some eat too much, some drink too much, and others go hungry. The love ethic has broken down. Theissen argues that this is not just a question of selfishness or lack of consideration on the part of some, but rather a reflection of social stratification as reflected in eating customs. He shows from convincing literary parallels about Greco-Roman dining habits that it was a familiar occurrence for those of upper class status to have or be served better food even in the presence of their social inferiors or dependents who had to make do with less food or poorer quality.

Evidently some in the Corinthian community have not quite caught on to the realistic implications of the Christian love ethic, but are continuing their ordinary discriminatory practices and indiscriminate imbibing even when meeting together for the solemn agape meal which will be climaxed by the eucharistic sharing of bread and cup in memory of Jesus' last meal with his disciples. What they have not realized and are doing violence to is the fact that "the sacramental act of the Lord's Supper is a symbolic accomplishment of social integration. From many people emerges a single entity."[14]

While Theissen has been criticized by Meeks and others for attempting to tie theological differences too closely to social status, his interpretations have on the whole been widely welcomed. They deserve to be received with the same caution as those of theologians, no less and no more. He has certainly done solid research and drawn provocative conclusions which cannot be ignored. He has demonstrated once again that theological conflicts do not exist independently of the social experiences and presuppositions of the persons involved.

In *The First Urban Christians,* Wayne Meeks more recently takes up many of the themes raised by Theissen and builds on his work and that of many others.[15] In an extensively documented book intended for the general reader, he portrays more thoroughly than Theissen the social and economic context of the Pauline communities. His first chapter on their urban environment recreates the world of the Greco-Roman city with its thriving commercial and intellectual life; its tradition of home rule by leading local families over against the pressures of Roman provincial administration; the effects of Roman military colonies in urban centers like Corinth or Philippi side by side with the traditional Greek population. The chapter highlights the way in which the cities grew progressively apart culturally from their surrounding villages and countryside as they entered the mainstream of a common urban culture, aesthetically Greek, administratively Roman.

The trade routes and commercial prosperity fostered the kind of geographical mobility for the business class which probably provided the context for much of the travel of Christians, as has already been mentioned. The upward social and economic mobility particularly of the freedman class provided a large group of the restless *nouveaux riches* very likely to be interested in new ideas and a new faith. The cities of the Pauline mission were port and market centers, military colonies and Roman provincial capitals. Many had large Jewish populations, whose synagogues according to Acts were the first centers for the missionary preaching of the apostles.

Meeks' second chapter again takes up the question of the social level of Christians in Pauline communities, already discussed above in regard to Theissen. Meeks generally accepts and summarizes the findings of Theissen, Judge, and others who have done extensive work with the meager information provided in the New Testament texts, but he presents the relevant material clearly and in interesting fashion. The case of the collection for Jerusalem in 2 Corinthians 8 and 9 is pointed out as an instance in which the language of abundance and poverty is used figuratively, certainly, but also with the exception that the Corinthians and Macedonians are quite able to give of their financial abundance; indeed Paul seems to be playing the two groups off against each other in the hope that a little competitive feeling will produce better results (compare 2 Cor 8:2–3; 9:2–4)! Meeks draws attention to the comments by which Paul seems to have expected help from the Corinthians for his travel expenses from their city to the next on his itinerary (the usual meaning of *propempein* which is used here: 1 Cor 16:6, 11; 2 Cor 1:16), quite the contrary of the blanket rejection he seems to make in 1 Corinthians 9:12–18 in regard to any kind of support from them.

The conclusions of Meeks' analysis of Christian social stratification generally agree with those of other recent scholars who have examined the evidence. With the exception of the extreme top and bottom of the social ladder, the Pauline communities are a cross section of Greco-Roman urban society. There are no members of the senatorial or equestrian *ordines* and probably none of the lowest levels: unskilled laborers, peasants, and the habitually destitute. But all the intermediate levels are represented: slaves, freedmen and freedwomen, artisans and traders, small business people and merchants, people with extensive households who function as patrons, perhaps even an occasional prominent local family.

Meeks finds that those who can be singled out as most active in Paul's circles are those with high "status inconsistency" and consequent low "status crystallization," people whose "achieved status" acquired by taking advantage of new opportunities in their path is higher than their "attributed status" determined by birth. These are the people who are feeling the pressure between what they have been and what they could become, between what they would like to be and what the social stratification will still deny them. He then rightly asks whether these are the people likely to be most receptive to a new message of salvation, equality, and hope, or whether they simply stand out in any group because of the particular characteristics of their behavior. A question well worth asking, to which we will never know the answer for sure.

Meeks' third chapter examines four models from the social environment which may have influenced the shape of the Christian *ekklēsia,* the assembly or church: the household, the voluntary association or club, the synagogue, and the philosophical school. All have been described at least briefly at the beginning of this chapter, and the household will be taken up again in Chapter 4 below. He then goes on to discuss the social function of boundaries in the Pauline community, using the categories of Victor Turner. The experience of social liminality is intended in Turner's schema as a transient and intermediate phase during a ritual of initiation, but is used here as a lasting state for those in eschatological preparedness. It leads to a warm, open, and egalitarian quality of relationship within the liminal group that Turner calls *communitas*. The boundaries which differentiate the group from the rest of society tend to reinforce their differentness. The stronger the boundaries, the stronger the inner sense of *communitas* and vice versa. While contrasting their own worldview to that of the outside world and therefore rejecting its structures, the group nevertheless necessarily creates its own alternative "anti-structures." Thus while insisting that Christian life is different and in some senses cut off from the world (e.g. the rejection of civil lawsuits for Christians in 1 Corinthians 6:1–6), nevertheless Paul insists on the maintenance of a decorum that would be acceptable even to outsiders (1 Cor 11:2–16; 14:23–35).

The language of separation in the Pauline writings reinforces the experience of liminality: while the insiders are the holy ones, those being saved, the others are unbelievers, the unrighteous, those who are perishing. There is not only a present social differentiation but a sequential one as well: those who were once enslaved to the powers of ignorance have now been set free in Christ. Since the body in any culture is an image of society, the treatment of the body in a culture will indicate the level of social control: tight control of purity regulations and bodily conduct is accompanied by a strict sense of in-group over against outsiders.[16] In Corinth different members of the community interpreted the boundaries differently with regard to eating meat sacrificed to idols (1 Cor 8 and 10); other differences of interpretation arose in regard to sexuality (1 Cor 6:12–7:7). With these questions as with those of community governing structure discussed in Meeks' fourth chapter, Paul's approach is to create strong boundaries of identity that are yet characterized by a certain freedom and flexibility in the application of rules.

The final chapters of Meeks' book pursue the function of ritual and patterns of belief in creating and sustaining the social world of Pauline Christians. The ritual of baptism is a "permanent threshold" through which the Christian enters a new order, a transition from darkness, ignorance, evil, the "dirty" world through the cleansing rite to light, knowledge, goodness, the "clean" new community. Divisions of social status are exchanged for unity in Christ, of which the ritual of Eucharist is the living expression; hence Paul's refusal in 1 Corinthians 11:17–22 to tolerate violation of its symbolism.

Patterns of belief in Pauline teaching reinforce group identity and solidarity: the community is the body of Christ set off from the world by its paradoxical exultation of the Crucified One; its expectation of his imminent return puts it in a state of ongoing liminality in which it proclaims the beginnings of a transition from bondage to liberation, estrangement to reconciliation, guilt to justification. The status inconsistency already experienced by many Pauline Christians in their social status is transformed into a vision of common unity, but the tension of the inconsistency is not obliterated but rather transferred to the eschatological dimension of expectation. The Christian is status–inconsistent in a new way, between the old and new creations.

Conclusion

We have traced some of the social factors operative in the life of Paul and in the churches he founded. The evidence as illumined by recent scholarship indicates gatherings of people from across the social spectrum, with the exception of the very lowest levels and the highest aristocratic orders. In a cosmopolitan world, the Christian communities represented a fairly typical social mix, which in itself was probably somewhat untypical for a social or religious organization.

Those of unequal social status were to treat each other as brothers and sisters in the Lord. When husband and wife, master and slave, patron and client belonged to the same house church, they were to express their unity in Christ by sharing the same table and dealing with one another with equal consideration. What of the rest of their lives? Were the same unity and equality of status to carry over into their everyday lives? Such ideas were potentially subversive and were probably already in Paul's day sowing the seeds of future trouble.

Part III
MALE AND FEMALE: FAMILY STRUCTURES AND CHURCH ORGANIZATION

5
Charism, Authority and Structure

In the previous chapter we looked at the early Christian communities as part of their world, and at the social life of Christians and how it reflected the ordinary life around them. Except for a few remarks about styles of Christian leadership garnered from Theissen and Meeks, we have yet to focus on the internal structure of Christian communities in the Pauline churches and beyond. Before looking at those aspects of the New Testament in which family relationships came to be an important element, let us first examine the earlier period in which Christianity suggested an alternative to the family.

It is commonly accepted by scholars that 1 Corinthians 12–14 is to be taken seriously as Paul's articulation of his ideal vision of community: the mutual respecting of each other's spiritual gifts freely and responsibly exercised; the priority of love over all; the importance of prophecy; the necessity of maintaining order in the assembly. The picture is one of freedom and spontaneity in a relatively unstructured religious gathering that is, however, already beginning to establish recognized procedures (e.g. 1 Cor 12:18; 14:26–35). Definite and permanent kinds of authority are not yet invested in local leaders (though the beginnings of this kind of government may already be discernible in the overseers and deacons of Philippians 1:1 and the deacon Phoebe in Romans 16:1–2).

Because the itinerant missionary apostles are the initiators of Christian life in the Diaspora, theirs is the earliest formulation of structures of authority. From the information to be gleaned predominantly from Acts and the Pauline letters, we can tentatively recon-

struct a network of authority among Paul and his apostolic companions. This has been done most recently by Bengt Holmberg in *Paul
and Power: The Structure of Authority in the Primitive Church as
Reflected in the Pauline Epistles.*

The first part of the book assembles and interprets the data in
three areas. The first area is Paul's relationship to the Jerusalem
church. Despite Paul's protest in Galatians 1 and 2 that he received
the Gospel he preaches not from human authority but directly from
the risen Christ, a close reading of even that passage reveals in Paul
a certain deference to those in Jerusalem with legitimate ties to the
historical Jesus: "I laid out privately to those who were qualified the
Gospel that I preach to the Gentiles, lest I go or had gone somehow
off on the wrong track" (Gal 2:3). Holmberg concludes that for Paul
the officials in Jerusalem have "status authority" in virtue of their
unique qualifications. Paul submits to their authority in two ways: by
seeking and accepting their authorization at the Jerusalem summit
meeting (also described in Acts 15), and by making the collection of
funds in the Greek churches and turning it over to the Jerusalem
church. Paul does this, Holmberg argues, not out of charity but as a
matter of ecclesiology, as a demonstration of the deference he felt was
owed by Gentile Christians to the "mother church."

The second area of data interpretation is the network of relationships among Paul and his co-workers.[1] From eighty to one hundred
(depending on how one interprets certain passages) are named in the
Pauline letters and Acts in some kind of cooperative association in
ministry. It is usually only through careful analysis of the language
that patterns and structures can be detected, i.e. Titus (2 Cor 8:6) and
Apollos (1 Cor 16:12) are "urged" while Timothy is "sent" (1 Thes
3:2; 1 Cor 4:17; Phil 2:19); Phoebe the deacon is "commended" as a
benefactor (Rom 16:1–2), while Barnabas is a respected leader, a
traveling companion and partner of Paul but never his subordinate. In
fact, Holmberg speculates that Paul may originally have been an
assistant of Barnabas before striking out independently (see Acts
11:24–26).

The third area of interpretation of Pauline authority is in the
local churches founded by Paul. Holmberg finds that here Paul has
personal authority because of the power of his own person and his
acknowledged holiness. He also has procedural or functional authority

by virtue of what he represents. As "their" founder and apostle he bears divine (though certainly not absolute) authority, and does not hesitate to wield it when a situation moves in a different direction than he would judge best.

Charism and Office

The more difficult issue in regard to authority in the local churches is the extent to which local leadership had already in Paul's day developed into what can later be clearly defined as "office," that is, "permanent acknowledged functions in local churches filled by stable groups of persons who lead and serve and take responsibility for their congregations in different ways, in some cases even having a designation or title and some form of material support."[2] Holmberg's conclusion is that even though according to this description the function is not yet fully developed, still we can rightly speak of such "office" in the Pauline churches.

It has been customary among early Church historians since the turn of the century to juxtapose or play off against one another as dialectically opposed forces the two factors of "charism" and "office." In this way of thinking "charism" is free, unstructured, prophetic leadership which derives its authority from the inspiration of the Spirit, and responds in an *ad hoc* manner to needs as they arise. "Office" then is permanent, stable leadership by designated individuals, founded on juridically constituted authority which is regularly transmitted in a hierarchical succession. Stereotypically put, charism means freedom and spontaneity; office means stability and continuity, and ultimately the suppression of charism under the weight of its authority. Thus the two factors represent opposite and irreconcilable poles, one of which was swallowed up and destroyed by the other in the course of early Church history. The charismatic church would then be represented by the authentic Pauline letters, especially Romans, Galatians, and 1 and 2 Corinthians, the official Church by the later, or deutero-Pauline letters, Colossians, Ephesians, 1 and 2 Timothy and Titus, and by such other later New Testament books as 1 and 2 Peter, James, and Jude, most of which seem to present the picture of a more stabilized church structure, sometimes referred to in this literature as "early Catholicism."

More recently this historical interpretation has been called into question as simplistic, and Holmberg's conclusion that one can properly speak of "office" already in the Pauline churches is typical of this trend. If "office" is already present in Paul's churches, it is equally true that "charism" does not disappear in the later, more institutionalized Church of the second and third centuries, since some of the most hierarchical authority figures of that period, e.g. Ignatius of Antioch and Cyprian of Carthage, consider themselves "charismatics" who possess the spirit of prophecy and live according to its inspiration. In short, though there is a definitely traceable development of institutionalization that takes place in the early Church and is already discernible in the New Testament, it cannot be blamed for the demise of charism.[3] The explanation of later developments is more complex. How then to explain it?

Sociology and Authority

Here is where sociological theory steps in. The second part of Holmberg's book builds on the exegetical conclusions of the first to elucidate the structure of authority in the earliest years of the Church by means of the theories of the well-known sociologist of religion, Max Weber. Weber understands authority as power to cause another to assent, not out of constraint but out of conviction. He distinguishes three types of authority or "legitimate domination:" charismatic, due to the exceptional characteristics of the person and/or a claim to supernatural revelation; traditional, based on established procedures and accepted legitimacy; rational-legal, resting on belief in the legality of rules and the rights of those who exercise authority under those rules.

What Weber documented and formulated into theory some years ago was the development of charismatic leadership into institutional leadership, the process whereby charism becomes traditionalized, rationalized, or both—the "routinization" of charism, as he called it. For Weber and for many Church historians, this development is a lamentable decline, even though probably inevitable if the group is to continue. Weber's observations apply to any social or religious movement which begins with the enthusiastic response of followers to a visionary leader. They are still helpful for understanding the origins of Christianity and of sub-groups within it throughout history, such as religious orders.

A problem arises when a negative value judgment about the development from charismatic to traditional/legal group, from sect to institution, prevails. Then there is a pristine Christianity which existed only for a brief period, perhaps one generation—that of Jesus and Paul. Once the powers of routinization and institutionalization set to work, the original impetus is diluted into something of secondary value: the time of the later New Testament and all subsequent generations, punctuated by periodic renewal movements which eventually suffer the same fate. It's a pretty bleak picture of religious history.

Holmberg takes up Weber's theory, applies it to the changes taking place in the Pauline churches, and suggests an alternative interpretation of the development from sect to institution. Rather than speaking of the routinization of charism, Holmberg proposes to understand the process as the transformation of charismatic leadership and structure into other types. This is especially relevant if the charismatic authority himself/herself is not the victim of institutionalization, but rather the intiator, as Holmberg finds Paul to be. When the charism seeks institutional manifestation for the sake of stability, order, and continuity, a new phase in the life of the movement is underway, neither better nor worse, but necessary for survival. The effects of this institutionalizing phenomenon move in two directions. First, there is more social control and less general freedom. Second, a different kind of freedom is created: freedom from the pressure and ambiguity of living in an unstructured world, and as a result further capacity for self-governed action.

Holmberg would describe the apostolic Church as an institutionalized charismatic movement, that is, a movement begun through the inspiration of a dynamic leader whose very person commanded authority and whose claim to revelation was compelling, a movement which subsequently followed the inevitable laws of nature for such groups by evolving structures and more permanent types of authority which responded to the ongoing need for ordering in a continuing existence. In the process, the charism is not lost, but transformed into different shapes and manifestations.

Weber's work has been criticized on minor points and on some of his interpretations of the overall implications of his theory. Its main lines remain valid. Holmberg's careful analysis and critique of Weber are an important contribution to the understanding of early Christianity. Not everyone will agree with his exegetical conclusions, especially his excessive dependence on Acts as historically reliable, at times even against Paul. Those who envision Paul as champion of unstructured freedom over against later Christian institutionalists will not approve of his attempt to demonstrate a well-ordered authority network in the first Christian generation. But here is a scholar who portrays the transition to institutionalized structure as beginning much earlier than many have thought, and he argues his point well, not out of denominational partisanship but from textual data and sociological theory.

What were some of the factors which prompted this institutionalizing development in the next generation after Paul? This will be the subject of the next chapter.

6
The Household Code
and Its Implications

One of the characteristics of many of the later books of the New Testament written in letter form is the tendency to encourage more definite structures of Church life. This has already been mentioned in the previous chapter. The descriptions of qualifications for bishops, deacons, widows, and presbyters in 1 Timothy 3:1–13 and 5:3–22 and Titus 1:5–9 are good examples which indicate early forms of established leadership roles. There is a particular literary form in this category which has recently been the subject of much interest from the perspective of social setting: the household code. This form consists of sets of mutually reciprocal duties among categories of people in the extended patriarchal household: usually husbands and wives, masters and slaves, parents and children. Examples are: Ephesians 5:21—6:9, Colossians 3:18—4:1 and 1 Peter 2:13—3:8. Note that not all passages contain exhortations for all six groups.

Recall what was said in Chapter 4 about the strong need for ordering in the Greco-Roman world, the importance of authority figures as guardians and preservers of that order, and the centrality of the extended family as the basic unit of society, after which, according to many ancient philosophers, the other basic social unit, the city-state, is modeled. It is time now to turn our attention to the structuring of this extended patriarchal family, its literary expression in the household code, and the significance of these social concepts for Christian life in the late first and early second century.

To know the origin of the household code is to know something of its history, social setting, and intention. Unfortunately, there is no agreement on its origins, and it represents a way of thinking that is very familiar in the ancient world. A recent book by David Balch, *Let Wives Be Submissive: The Domestic Code in 1 Peter,* explores the possible origins and function of the household code particularly in 1 Peter in a way that highlights the social setting and real circumstances behind its use in one New Testament letter.

Balch's exploration of the origins of the household code leads him to reject prior theories of its beginnings in Jewish ethical teaching or philosophers contemporary to the New Testament writers. Rather, he finds it to be a literary theme traceable at least as far back as Plato and Aristotle, though it was probably already old in their day. There are two familiar and related topics for philosophical discourse traceable at least that far back: On Household Management and On the Constitution, that is, on the essential and ideal ingredients for both domestic and political prosperity and harmony. Discussion of these interrelated topics continues through the philosophical treatises and ethical manuals of the Hellenistic period and on into Roman times.

The two topics are interrelated precisely because of the concept articulated by Plato and followed by many others including the first century Jewish philosopher Philo—that the household is a microcosm of the state, or, put differently, the state is a macrocosm of the household. Thus maintenance of order in one is integral to maintenance of order in the other; subversion in one means inevitable subversion in the other. The quality of harmony in the state is then intimately dependent on the harmony of the family. Disruption of family patterns means disruption of the political process and vice versa (compare the nineteenth and twentieth century fear that the granting of equal rights to women is injurious to the family). The patriarchal family head, the *paterfamilias* in Roman terminology, cannot govern in the civil sphere if he cannot govern in the domestic sphere (compare the church leader in 1 Timothy 3:4–5 who cannot manage a church if he cannot manage his household). In many of these passages, the same triple dyadic pattern is present as in the New Testament household codes: husband-wife, master-slave, parent-child.

It is interesting to note that Aristotle objected to the comparison of household and state in regard to the exercise of authority, for he considered the style of household authority too harsh and severe to be extrapolated to the political sphere. While in practice he was probably correct, in theory the Platonic association and interrelationship of the two continued to exercise tremendous influence in the literature of several centuries.

Implicit in this association, of course, is the assumption that good order requires a hierarchical pattern of dominance and submission not only with regard to children and slaves, but also with regard to wives. While the legal treatment of women varied from region to region and from generation to generation in the ancient world, never in Greco-Roman or Jewish society did women enjoy full legal status. They were always in some way under the protection and dominance of male authority. The actual exercise of this dominance may have taken the severe form of the right of life and death on the part of the *paterfamilias* in early republican Rome, or the apparently extensive independence enjoyed by women under Roman law to conduct their own business, legal, and social transactions during the years of the Empire. But women's status as legal persons never equaled that of men.

While philosophers disputed whether or not men and women had the same nature and the same capacity for virtue, the notion that the public domain belonged properly to men and the domestic domain to women was prevalent and considered the ideal. Exceptions were notable, scarce, and often legendary. As independent as some upper-class women of imperial Rome may have been, none ever held government positions. In spite of good evidence to the contrary, the ideal virtuous woman proposed by male writers was shy, retiring, and happy to remain secluded at home, occupied with domestic management and weaving.[1]

Even those philosophers who argued for equality of nature between men and women seem to have seen no contradiction between affirming equality of nature and inequality of social roles. This contradiction was apparently not widely recognized until modern times. Wives, slaves, and children are the three groups in the Roman world from whom submission was required. And if the dominance-submission pattern was not really questioned between men and women, it is not surprising that the *institution* of slavery (as distinct from its abuse) was not widely questioned on philosophical or humanitarian grounds, either. What becomes noticeably different in the New Testament codes is the exhortation to *mutual* submission on the part of all (e.g. Eph. 5:21).

Function of the Code in 1 Peter

The household code of 1 Peter 2:13—3:8 has several peculiarities. First, it is introduced by an exhortation to everyone to submit to all legitimate political authority as to God (2:13–17). Second, parents and children are completely lacking, and the order of the remaining two sets is reversed. Third, there is no exhortation to masters, and the verses devoted to slaves are expanded into a commentary on the sufferings of Christ that is explicitly patterned after parts of the suffering servant passage of Isaiah 53, seeming to tell slaves to bear all suffering patiently in memory of the suffering Christ. Fourth, the exhortation to wives goes so far as to encourage *obedience* to husbands (3:6) after the example of Sarah to Abraham, a doubtful exegesis of the intention of Genesis 18:12. Fifth, the beginning of the exhortation to wives (3:1) leaves a telltale sign of possible social conflict: the virtuous submission of wives to their husbands may bring about the husbands' conversion to the faith.

Balch draws on the comparative evidence of Greek mystery cults, and the accusations leveled indiscriminately against them, against Judaism, and against Christianity as well, of secret nocturnal meetings full of immorality, of disruption of familial concord by encouragement of individual conversions from either sex and any legal status without approval of the proper patriarchal authority. These independent decisions of conversion naturally implied further ongoing independent activity (attendance at meetings and worship services and daily personal prayer) which was seen by many as a serious threat to the stability of the family. Disparity of worship within a household was already a problem. Disparity of worship between husband and wife was crucial; one of the ideals proposed by the writers on marriage and household management was that, no matter what gods a young woman was accustomed to worship in her parents' house, she should forsake them at marriage and worship only those of her husband. Encouraging wives and slaves to think independently and accept the authority of someone other than the male householder was indeed subversion of domestic order and therefore of civil order, a sufficient cause for resentment and persecution.

At this point let us recall some of the impressions we can gather of the earlier Pauline communities, where the family unit is the Body of Christ, the community with its many members, where authority is claimed by apostles, prophets, and teachers (1 Cor 12:28), not by heads of households. There the Christian community really functions as an *alternative* to the household. Paul will sometimes speak in patriarchal terms (Phil 2:22; 1 Thes 2:11; 1 Cor 4:14–15) since this is a familiar idiom in his society, but he does not go about setting up communities governed by the type of hierarchical paternal authority typical of the household of the day. Nevertheless, the power of the apostle vis-à-vis his congregation is a definite authority over persons who also belong to households in which the patriarchal head may or may not also be Christian (read 1 Corinthians 7:12–16, 20–24 on wives and slaves from this perspective). When he is not, patterns of suspicion and resentment are no doubt present.

Balch proposes that it is in answer to just such a situation that the author of 1 Peter writes his household code. It aims to show that in every possible respect, Christians conform to the expectations of society: slaves are humble and obedient even when unjustly punished; wives are chaste, simple, and submissive. Their faith need not be a threat to the social status quo. The household code in 1 Peter therefore functions as a defensive apologetic answer to slanderous accusation of misconduct. If Christianity is accused of disrupting the social order, especially through conversions of wives and slaves, it is those very groups who are in the strongest terms urged to live exemplary lives in all other respects. The code is a document which can be cited to show outsiders that Christians really stand for order, whatever contrary rumors may be circulating. At the same time, it instructs Christians, especially wives and slaves of pagan husbands and masters, who are in the most vulnerable position, how to behave in order to appease those in power. Hope is even held out that the good example of Christian wives may convert their husbands, though that was probably too much to hope for in the case of slaves.

The Church as Household

Another and more extensive recent study of 1 Peter approaches the form and function of the letter somewhat differently. John H. Elliott's *A Home for the Homeless: A Sociological Exegesis of 1 Peter,*

Its Situation and Strategy attempts to develop a method called by the author "sociological exegesis." By combining interpretations from the historical-critical method and models from the social sciences, Elliott seeks to correlate the literary, sociological, and theological aspects of the text as well as its intended impact, which he calls the author's "strategy."

Elliott calls attention to some of the peculiar language of 1 Peter which situates it in its contemporary world, where the present existence of Christians is called their *paroikia* (1:17), and they themselves are referred to as *paroikoi* (2:11) and *parepidēmoi* (1:1; 2:11). In the legal terminology of the ancient Greek world, the *paroikos* (Latin equivalent: *peregrinus*) is a resident alien permanently without rights of citizenship because of status by birth, just as citizenship in a city is restricted to those born into families with the legal status of citizen. The *parapidēmos* is one with even less status, a visiting stranger with no permanent habitation in the political entity. Thus the associations of impermanence, transiency, and exile are attached to the terms.

Elliott goes further in attempting to situate the actual social setting of the letter. The addressees of 1:1 belong to central and northern Asia Minor (present-day Turkey), a largely rural area though not without its urban centers. He calls attention to the rural imagery used in the letter (e.g. 1:22–24; 2:25; 5:2–4) and draws upon available historical evidence of the disintegrating situation of the rural laboring classes of Asia Minor to suggest that the language of temporary residential status may be more actual than figurative, that a real social situation of legal contingency and increasing economic hardship leads the author to use the exile theme as a way of understanding the community's theological status as comparable to its civil status, an idea already in common use (e.g. Phil 3:20; Heb 13:14). At the same time, typical language of urban life, like Paul's *ekklēsia* (assembly of citizens) and *politeuma* (citizenship in a political entity—cf. Phil 3:20) are notably absent. He therefore concludes that the predominant audience of 1 Peter comes from the rural peasant class.

Elliott then introduces a series of characteristics of religious sects as compiled by cross-cultural observation and analysis according to social science method: tension with the external world, disillusionment with the social situation, definite internal procedures and expectations, voluntary membership, egalitarian ideals, and future-oriented stance.

The sect's biggest tension is between its open mission orientation, born of the conviction of the rightness and goodness of its positions, and the necessity to close out the external world to preserve internal cohesion. The sociological result of conflict is the necessity to reinforce group identity and cohesion for the sake of the survival and health of the movement.

Since the days of Max Weber early Christianity has been studied sociologically under the category of the sect. Thus Elliott argues that most of the above characteristics can be seen in 1 Peter. In the face of persecution, clearly alluded to in the letter (3:13–17; 4:12–19; 5:10), the author's strategy is to reinforce group cohesion by stressing internal coherence over against the external world. The readers are encouraged not to become but to remain what they already are, socially as well as theologically: resident aliens. By not playing on the "heavenly home" theme as do Philippians 3:20 and Hebrews 13:14, the author of 1 Peter reveals the link with the readers' social-legal status: they are not to "put on" a notion of impermanence for the sake of eschatology; rather, they are to make sense, in light of their faith, of the real situation they face. There is no escapism here.

Within this internally coherent community, the operant model is the household, not because of the Church's assimilation to societal models (as argued by Balch), but as an alternative household of God which operates not by human standards but by divine ones. In support of this interpretation is the recurrent household language of the letter. The community is to be built into a spiritual household (2:5), the household of God (4:17), in which all are house servant-stewards (4:10), and husbands live together with their wives in domestic harmony (3:7). In the household code, the usual word for slaves, *douloi,* is replaced by *oiketai,* specifically house slaves. Though it may not be clear in the various English translations, each of the passages cited above uses in Greek some form or compound of *oikos,* house or household.

Elliott therefore argues that 2:5–10, whose language of priesthood and sacrifice is usually understood as figurative appropriation of Jewish worship into the beginnings of a notion of Christian cultic sacrifice, is not meant to be cultic language at all, but rather a movement from temple to household as the model of the Christian structure of worship.[2]

Here we must again recall what has been said previously about the importance of the household as the basic social unit. The city and the Empire are structured along similar lines; the emperor is *pater patriae,* father of the fatherland; his vast administrative network of civil servants is known as the *familia Caesaris,* and patriotism means loyalty to the patriarchal system. In Elliott's view the Church of 1 Peter does not copy all this, but rather provides an alternative in recognizable form, the household of God which operates according to radically different principles.

In the household code of 1 Peter therefore, servants unexpectedly are mentioned first and longest for a theological reason, because they best exemplify the household concept (not because their conversion is the biggest public relations problem as Balch would have it). But the servants of the code are not merely literal servants. They are the paradigm of all Christians and especially of those who suffer. The wives of pagan husbands are not only literally so, but also symbols of the gentleness, patience, and submission by which Christians will be accepted by pagans and win them over. The crisis faced by the community is not in Elliott's view one of blatant and open persecution but rather the result of more subtle kinds of pressure and oppression which Christians are experiencing within their daily lives and even in the heart of their families. Reinforcement of the internal cohesion of the community provides the security its members need to persevere in faith and hope—a home for the homeless where they can reaffirm their true identity and create kinship ties that go deeper than blood relationship.

Elliott's reconstruction of the situation and strategy of 1 Peter is a much vaster understanding than the work of Balch. It is an enormous step forward toward an understanding of the letter, and has been generally well received. Criticisms usually center around three areas. First, the missionary strategy, the other side of sectarian cohesiveness, is neglected, and it too must be taken into account for a full understanding of the letter; the author is not closed into his own world. Second, the interpretation of the social situation is pushed too far: such rural imagery as appears in 1 Peter is commonplace and does not necessarily indicate an agrarian setting; the *paroikos* language must be seen in the context of other examples of figurative literary use of legal terminology without indication of corresponding social status, e.g.

Paul's frequent description of himself as a slave which in no way suggests for him the legal condition of slavery. Such figurative use of legal terms is also well known from non-Christian sources of the period.

The third criticism deals with the whole method involved. Elliott sets out to produce an analysis that interweaves sociological with historical, literary, and exegetical method. He succeeds well in the use of various methods side by side, but not in combining and melding them, particularly the social sciences, the inclusion of which is the new frontier. The introduction of sociological data and analysis does not in itself produce a "sociological exegesis." Nevertheless, Elliott has put forth a bold attempt that breaks new ground in the use of social science method in the study of early Christian literature and life.

Social Science Becomes Social Critique

The interpretations of Balch and Elliott open up new possibilities for situating 1 Peter as well as other later New Testament writings within their social contexts and early Christian history and theology. What neither writer has taken account of are the implications of the adoption of the household by Christian groups already near the end of the first century as the primary model of Christian relationship. Whether the motive was social adaptation to enhance acceptance and conversion as argued by Balch, or the creation of the alternative household of God as proposed by Elliott, the effect is the same. The household structure is canonized, and with it the patriarchal pattern of dominance and submission which it implies.

Fatherhood becomes the model for the exercise of authority in the Church, and the submission of wives and obedience of slaves and children the models for response to that authority. The household codes convey a deeply challenging invitation to the *loving* exercise of authority and obedience, but their proponents do not question the appropriateness of the patriarchal structure itself as a model for Christian relationship.

Theissen and Troeltsch before him speak of "love-patriarchalism" as the foundational ethic of early Christian communities. Under this concept equality of status in Christ belongs to all regardless of social status. But "in the political and social realm class-specific differences were essentially accepted, affirmed, even religiously legitimated."[3] The difference for Christians was the emphasis on mutual love as the mode of relationship within the given hierarchically structured society. For Balch and Theissen the conflict was created by the tension between two principles difficult to harmonize: patriarchy and equality of freedom in Christ. For Elliott that tension seems to resolve into the love-patriarchalism of a community that sees itself as the household of God.

But is the tension really resolved so easily? This assumption of early Christians' willing acceptance of a social theology of inequality is being questioned from the perspective of liberation critique, most recently by Elisabeth Schüssler Fiorenza, *In Memory of Her: A Feminist Theological Reconstruction of Christian Origins*. By viewing early Christianity as a *social* reality, Fiorenza is able to utilize a formidable amount of the social history and social science research into Christian origins to challenge centuries-long assumptions about the inherent patriarchalism of the tradition from its earliest years. For both Theissen and Fiorenza, the teaching and attitude of Jesus represent an alternative approach open to the equality of all under the sole authority of God. While Theissen would see the principle of love-patriarchalism already operative in the Pauline churches and Paul's own teachings, Fiorenza posits its Christian beginnings only in the later New Testament writings, though she concedes that the language of fatherhood sometimes used by Paul (e.g. 1 Cor 4:15, 17, 21; 2 Cor 11:2-3; Phil 2:22) opens the way toward the subsequent return of Christians to the patriarchal model.

Fiorenza suggests status dissonance—the anomaly of possessing different levels of status at the same time—as motivation for the large numbers of women who joined religious groups and private clubs, synagogues and Christian assemblies. In the household they were structurally and legally inferior even though as wives or widows of the well-to-do they may have exercised a great deal of independence and authority over others. Private associations and minority religious groups not organized along the lines of the dominant social structure gave them the experience of freedom and respect that they had tasted but that was officially denied to them elsewhere.

The Pauline churches would have provided just such an experience, in which the reality of individual charisms was affirmed regardless of legal status, ethnic origins, or sex (Gal 3:28), even though in specific local situations Paul may not have been as totally consistent with his principles as some would have liked (e.g. 1 Cor 11:2–16; 14:34–35 if this passage is authentically Pauline). Later New Testament writers see patriarchalism as a social and political necessity for the maintenance of order. Ephesians, Colossians, and the Pastoral Epistles use the household codes to reinforce the patriarchal model within the community itself; 1 Peter may use it for external propaganda (Balch) but also for internal use (Elliott) because notions of equality are seen as a threat to the social order itself—an idea that is at least as old as Plato and Aristotle.

Liberation social critique reaffirms the primary Christian egalitarian vision as reconstructed by social science method and social history. It calls for the re-creation of an alternative social model which will respect that original vision and call together a community of mutuality, in which patterns of domination and submission are overcome by love and full personhood is able to be realized by all.

Fiorenza and others[4] represent the cutting edge of the merger of social science method and liberation theology, one of the important directions in which social study of the Bible is moving. The social scientists and social historians can highlight their findings in regard to the diversity and adaptability of early Christian structures and ideals. It is then up to biblical theologians to interpret these findings and their significance for our life today. If biblical religion's prophetic proclamation of freedom and liberation to the suffering and oppressed is to mean anything beyond historical data, it must take on this added dimension.

Conclusion

There are many different ways to approach the New Testament. At one extreme one can be totally unconcerned about its impact on our times and be completely caught up in its historical data and its ideas as witness to the thinking of a religious sect of twenty centuries ago. At the opposite extreme one can almost completely ignore the ways in which the life described in the New Testament differs from ours, and care only about the "timeless truths" contained in it as if the meaning of the verbal expression of people in a different culture two thousand years ago could correspond exactly to that of a modern technologized culture. Obviously neither extreme is very wise.

All biblical study is located somewhere on the spectrum between these two points. The current method of social study of the New Testament makes one kind of contribution to the attempt to bridge the gap between "then" and "now" by proposing cross-cultural models of human interaction and methods for analysis of social information that can be comprehensible in a variety of social settings. Of course it must be recognized that no interpreter and no method of interpretation are completely objective, so that no matter how stringent the procedure, it is impossible to completely escape our own presuppositions and prejudices. But that is no reason to give up the attempt to continually refine the process.

In this volume we have discussed the findings of the social study of the New Testament as classified into the three major aspects of social relationship: ethnicity, status, and sex. The baptismal formula of Galatians 3:28 already expresses awareness of those divisions and the hope that, while remaining realities of life, they can in Christ cease to be divisive.

We have seen how the first Christian generations had to struggle with problems not too different from our own in the blending of cultures necessitated by the move from rural Palestinian to urban Greek environment. Within the first years after the death of Jesus his disciples were already facing the problems of cultural adaptation and ethnic differences.

Likewise the sharp social distinctions of class and status and the economic ambiguities of that world, placed in juxtaposition to an egalitarian vision that would provide a new and radical dimension to human relationships, produced another set of problems as Christianity struggled to be part of its world while yet retaining its distinctiveness.

Finally the need to formulate structures of internal Church life, and the way in which those structures impinged on the exercise of authority and freedom, posed more problems. The interrelatedness of sex roles and patterns of dominance in a heavily patriarchal society clashed with egalitarian impulses springing from the Christian vision.

The exploration of social expectations, patterns of relationship, and societal structures through the eyes of modern social science research method has its gaps and weaknesses. Its strength lies in its ability to illuminate for us not only complex patterns of behavior and relationship, but also the simple structures of everyday life upon which a society is built.

Thus the New Testament can be illuminated more closely as not only divine revelation about God, but also divine revelation to us about ourselves and the people of faith who have gone before us. We can too easily lose sight of the humanness of the Scriptures because it reminds us of our frailty. The Word of God can be communicated to us only in human language. The social study of the New Testament can help us to better understand that language.

Notes

Introduction

1. *The Sociology of Religion* (Beacon, 1963; original German publication, 1922); S.N. Eisenstadt, ed., *Max Weber on Charisma and Institution Building: Selected Papers* (University of Chicago, 1968).

2. *The Social Teaching of the Christian Churches,* 2 vols. (Harper, 1960; original German publication, 1912).

3. *Purity and Danger: An Analysis of Concepts of Pollution and Taboo* (Routledge and Kegan Paul, 1966); *Natural Symbols: Explorations in Cosmology* (Pantheon, 1970).

4. *The Sacred Canopy: Elements of a Sociological Theory of Religion* (Doubleday, 1967); P. Berger and T. Luckmann, *The Social Construction of Reality: A Treatise on the Sociology of Knowledge* (Doubleday, 1966).

5. *The Ritual Process* (Aldine, 1969). For an example of use of Turner with the New Testament, see George S. Worgul, "Anthropological Consciousness and Biblical Theology," *Biblical Theology Bulletin* 9 (1979), pp. 3–12.

6. Notably: J.Z. Smith, "The Social Description of Early Christianity," *Religious Studies Review* 1 (1975), pp. 19–25; D.J. Harrington, "Social Concepts in the Early Church: A Decade of Research," *Theological Studies* 41 (1980), pp. 181–190; R. Scroggs, "The Sociological Interpretation of the New Testament: The Present State of Research," *New Testament Studies* 26 (1980), pp. 164–179; H.C. Kee, *Christian Origins in Sociological Perspective: Methods and Resources* (Westminster, 1980). Two more recent and less technical articles have appeared in *Interpretation* 37:3 (July 1980); B.J. Malina, "The Social Sciences and Biblical Interpretation," pp. 229–242; J.G. Gager, "Shall We Marry Our Enemies? Sociology and the New Testament," pp. 256–265.

Chapter 1

1. For recent up-to-date material on archeological evidence for Herodian Jerusalem, both abundantly illustrated, see R. Mackowski, *Jerusalem, City of Jesus* (Eerdmans, 1980) and J. Wilkinson, *Jerusalem as Jesus Knew It: Archeology as Evidence* (Thames and Hudson, 1978). A thorough scholarly study of the history of Caesarea is *Caesarea Under Roman Rule* by L. J. Levine (Studies in Judaism in Late Antiquity 7; Brill, 1975). The results of the past ten years of archeological work at Caesarea are attractively described and illustrated by R.J. Bull, "Caesarea Maritima—The Search for Herod's City" and R.L. Hohlfedler, "Caesarea Beneath the Sea," both in *Biblical Archeology Review* 8:3 (May/June 1982), pp. 24–47.

2. M. Hengel, *Judaism and Hellenism,* Vol. 1, pp. 107–175.

3. *Ibid.,* pp. 243–247.

4. For the stories of Sepphoris and Tiberias, see Freyne, *Galilee,* pp. 122–134.

5. Freyne, *Galilee,* pp. 138–145.

6. Pp. 85–109.

7. See J.H. Leon, *The Jews of Ancient Rome* (Jewish Publication Society of America, 1960).

8. For a clear, straightforward introduction to Philo, see S. Sandmel, *Philo of Alexandria: An Introduction* (Oxford University, 1979).

9. For a more developed discussion of the main lines of these points, see Hengel, *Jews, Greeks, and Barbarians,* pp. 51–82.

Chapter 2

1. See for instance A.R. Hands, *Charities and Social Aid in Greece and Rome* (Cornell University, 1968), especially pp. 26–61.

2. *Time,* July 19, 1982, pp. 21–22.

3. "The Apostle Paul and the Introspective Conscience of the West," *Harvard Theological Review* 56 (1963), pp. 199–215; reprinted in *Paul Among Jews and Gentiles* (Fortress, 1976).

4. See Malina, *The New Testament World,* pp. 62–67 for numerous examples.

5. For archeological evidence of small farming in the neighborhood of ancient Jerusalem, see "Ancient Jerusalem's Rural Food Basket," by G. Edelstein and S. Gibson, *Biblical Archeology Review* 8:4 (July/August 1982), pp. 46–54.

6. For a well-illustrated, readable, though not sufficiently critical presentation of the mystery religions (including chapters on Judaism and Chris-

tianity) see J. Godwin, *Mystery Religions in the Ancient World* (Harper and Row, 1981).

Chapter 3

1. *Galilee,* pp. 194–200.
2. Especially P. Worsley, *The Trumpet Shall Sound. A Study of "Cargo" Cults in Melanesia* (Schocken, 1968), and K. Burridge, *New Heaven, New Earth: A Study of Millenarian Activities* (Schocken, 1969). As Gager notices, both titles are inspired by New Testament apocalypticism, yet neither book deals with early Christianity.
3. *Kingdom and Community,* p. 57, n. 1.
4. As developed especially by L. Festinger, H.W. Riecken, and S. Schachter, *When Prophecy Fails: A Social and Psychological Study of a Modern Group That Predicted the Destruction of the World* (Harper and Row, 1956) and L. Festinger, *A Theory of Cognitive Dissonance* (Stanford University, 1957).
5. German *Soziologie der Jesusbewegung* (Chr. Kaiser, 1977); English tr. by John Bowden (Fortress, 1978).

Chapter 4

1. "Peter and Paul," a CBS television production sponsored by Procter and Gamble, April 12 and 14, 1981.
2. Information about the Roman social order is readily available. A useful summary appears in Gager, *Kingdom and Community,* pp. 94–106, part of a revised version of a chapter entitled "Religion and Social Class in the Early Roman Empire" in Benko, *The Catacombs and the Colosseum,* pp. 99–120. A more extended and technical treatment is the superb chapter on "Orders and Status" in M.I. Finley, *The Ancient Economy* (U. of California, 1973), pp. 35–61. The next chapter, "Masters and Slaves," pp. 62–94, is also helpful for the present discussion.
3. Epictetus, *Discourses* 4.1. 33–40, available in Loeb Classical Library, tr. by W.A. Oldfather (Harvard U., 1966), Vol. 2, pp. 253–257.
4. For further helpful discussions of these and other characteristics of Greco-Roman society, see Meeks, *The First Urban Christians,* Chapter 1, pp. 9–50.
5. For a discussion of the relationship of literary culture to social status, see A. Malherbe, *Social Aspects of Early Christianity,* pp. 29–59.
6. "Paul's Tentmaking and the Problem of His Social Class," *Journal*

of Biblical Literature 97 (1978), pp. 555–564.

7. See M. Hengel, *Property and Riches in the Early Church,* Chapter 8, "The Ideal of 'Self-Sufficiency,'" pp. 54–59.

8. *Light from the Ancient East* (Baker, 1978; original German edition, 1908) and *Paul: A Study in Social and Religious History,* 2nd ed. (Harper and Row, 1957; original German edition, 1911). Many of these non-literary papyrus texts are available in *The New Testament Background: Selected Documents,* ed. C.K. Barrett (Harper and Row, 1961), pp. 23–47.

9. *The Social Pattern of Christian Groups in the First Century* (Tyndale, 1960)

10. Theissen's book is actually the collection and translation of a number of essays which appeared in German in 1974 and 1975. The introduction by John H. Schütz is very helpful for background and context. In addition, see the excellent collection of texts and historical information in *St. Paul's Corinth: Texts and Archeology* by J. Murphy-O'Connor (Michael Glazier, 1983).

11. Theissen, *Social Setting,* p. 15, in the introduction by J. Schütz.

12. Meeks, *First Urban Christians,* p. 2.

13. The two letters preserved are probably not the only ones Paul wrote to the Corinthians (see 1 Cor 5:9), and it is generally thought by scholars that the present 2 Corinthians is an amalgamation of as many as five shorter letters. But these are literary questions which need not concern us here.

14. Theissen, *Social Setting,* p. 167.

15. A synthesis of the conclusions and main ideas of Meeks' book appears as "The Social Context of Pauline Theology" in *Interpretation* 37:3 (1982), pp. 266–277.

16. Mary Douglas, *Natural Symbols,* quoted in Meeks, *First Urban Christians,* p. 97.

Chapter 5

1. Another earlier and very helpful study on this subject is that of E. Earle Ellis, "Paul and His Co-Workers," *New Testament Studies* 20 (1974), pp. 128–144.

2. Holmberg. *Paul and Power,* p. 111; a summary of the thinking of several other authors.

3. The whole issue of charism and office is much more complicated but cannot be further pursued here. For more discussion, see Holmberg, *Paul and Power,* pp. 95–121, with innumerable further references; also John H. Schütz, *Paul and the Anatomy of Apostolic Authority* (Cambridge U., 1975); John H. Elliott, "A Catholic Gospel: Reflections on 'Early Catholi-

cism' in the New Testament," *Catholic Biblical Quarterly* 31 (1969), pp. 213–223; Daniel J. Harrington, "The 'Early Catholic' Writings of the New Testament: The Church Adjusting to World-History," in *The Word in the World,* ed. R. Clifford and G. MacRae (Weston College Press, 1973); Carolyn Osiek, "The Relation of Charism to Rights and Duties in the New Testament Church," *The Jurist* 41 (1981), pp. 295–313, reprinted in *Official Ministry in a New Age,* ed. J. H. Provost (Permanent Seminar Studies 3; Washington: Canon Law Society of America/Catholic University, 1981), pp. 41–59.

Chapter 6

1. The topic of the role and status of women in the Greco-Roman world has been the subject of much recent research, sparked as much by recent societal and ecclesiastical changes as by scholarly interest. For more reading, the following are especially recommended: J.P.V.D. Balsdon, *Roman Women: Their History and Habits* (John Day Co., 1963; reprint: Barnes and Noble, 1983); Mary R. Lefkowitz and Maureen B. Fant, eds., *Women's Life in Greece and Rome: A Source Book in Translation* (Johns Hopkins, 1982); Moshe Meiselman, *Jewish Woman in Jewish Law* (KTAV, 1978); Sarah B. Pomeroy, *Goddesses, Whores, Wives and Slaves: Women in Classical Antiquity* (Schocken, 1975); Leonard Swidler, *Women in Judaism* (Scarecrow, 1976).

2. The interpretation of 1 Peter 2:5–10 is based on the conclusions of an earlier book by Elliott, *The Elect and the Holy: An Exegetical Examination of 1 Peter 2:4-10 and the Phrase* BASILEION HIERATEUMA (royal priesthood), Supplements to *Novum Testamentum* 12 (E.J. Brill, 1966). Here he argues that the priesthood language of the passage, based chiefly on Exodus 19:6, has no association with the Israelite priesthood and temple cult, but rather refers to the special consecration of Israel, and hence the Church, as God's holy people.

3. G. Theissen, *The Social Setting of Pauline Christianity,* p. 109; see further pp. 11, 37, 118, 138–139, 164.

4. Other recent examples include J. Severino Croatto, *Exodus: A Hermeneutics of Freedom* (Orbis, 1981) and Norman K. Gottwald, ed., *The Bible and Liberation: Political and Social Hermeneutics,* rev. ed., (Orbis, 1983), containing essays by Elliott, Fiorenza, Malina, Theissen, and others.

Suggestions for Further Study

Balch, David L. *Let Wives Be Submissive: The Domestic Code in 1 Peter*. Society of Biblical Literature: Scholars Press, 1981. A fascinating historical, literary, and social study of the origins of the household code and its function in 1 Peter.

Benko, Stephen and John J. O'Rourke. *The Catacombs and the Colosseum: The Roman Empire as the Setting of Primitive Christianity*. Valley Forge, PA: Judson, 1971. A helpful collection of studies on various social aspects of life in the early Roman Empire and how they may have influenced early Christianity.

Bruce, F.F. *New Testament History*. New York: Doubleday, 1971. An excellent summary of the historical background to the New Testament that is solid but not too heavy.

Elliott, John H. *A Home for the Homeless: A Sociological Exegesis of 1 Peter. Its Situation and Strategy*. Philadelphia: Fortress, 1981. A thorough study of the place and function of 1 Peter in the early Church and its intended effects in answer to specific social problems of Christian conversion.

Fiorenza, Elisabeth Schüssler. *In Memory of Her: A Feminist Theological Reconstruction of Christian Origins*. New York: Crossroad, 1983. In spite of the title, neither exclusively feminist nor exclusively theological, but rather a bold new attempt to blend exegesis, sociology, history and theology in retelling the story of Christian origins from a feminist perspective.

Freyne, Sean. *Galilee from Alexander the Great to Hadrian, 323 B.C.E. to 135 C.E.: A Study of Second Temple Judaism*. Wilmington, DE: Michael Glazier, and Notre Dame: University of Notre Dame, 1980. Extensively documented, scholarly study of the social and economic life of Galilee in New Testament times.

Freyne, Sean. *The World of the New Testament*. New Testament Message 2; Wilmington, DE: Michael Glazier, 1980. A good combination of historical, political, and social data in popular form.

Gager, John G. *Kingdom and Community: The Social World of Early Christianity*. Englewood Cliffs. NJ: Prentice-Hall, 1975. One of the first serious attempts to apply sociological theory to early Christianity.

Grant, Robert M. *Early Christianity and Society*. San Francisco: Harper and Row, 1977. Seven enlightening essays on cultural and economic aspects of the Roman world and what we know of Christians' part in them.

Hengel, Martin. *Judaism and Hellenism*. 2 vols. Philadelphia: Fortress, 1974. Extensive, detailed, scholarly, ground-breaking analysis of the influence of Greek civilization on Palestine. *Jews, Greeks, and Barbarians: Aspects of the Hellenization of Judaism in the Pre-Christian Period*. Philadelphia: Fortress, 1980. Much smaller but no less thorough continuation of *Judaism and Hellenism* with further insights and some extension to the Diaspora.

Hengel, Martin. *Property and Riches in the Early Church: Aspects of a Social History of Early Christianity*. Philadelphia: Fortress, 1974. A brief, clearly-written study of the early Christian attitude toward wealth, with contemporary problems very much in mind.

Hock, Ronald R. *The Social Context of Paul's Ministry: Tentmaking and Apostleship*. Philadelphia: Fortress, 1980. A brief and interesting investigation of the social context of Paul's trade and his insistence on refusing support from most of the communities which he founded.

Holmberg, Bengt. *Paul and Power: The Structure of Authority in the Primitive Church as Reflected in the Pauline Epistles*. Philadelphia: Fortress, 1980. A tightly-knit historical and sociological investigation of patterns of authority in the first generation of Christian missionaries.

Kee, Howard C. *Christian Origins in Sociological Perspective: Methods and Resources*. Philadelphia: Westminster, 1980. An inclusive summary treatment, with ample documentation, of the major categories helpful for a sociological interpretation of the New Testament: worldview, leadership and authority, identity, the role of religion and culture, the social function of the New Testament writings themselves.

Malherbe, Abraham J. *Social Aspects of Early Christianity*. Second Edition. Philadelphia: Fortress, 1983. Several pithy essays on the social background and its possible influences on early Christian educational and ecclesial life.

Malina, Bruce J. *The New Testament World: Insights from Cultural Anthropology*. Atlanta: John Knox, 1981. Remarkably lucid explanation of some major anthropological insights applied to the biblical world. Very readable, intended for college students.

Meeks, Wayne. *The First Urban Christians: The Social World of the Apostle Paul*. New Haven and London: Yale U., 1983. A massively detailed investigation of the urban world, social status and internal life of the Pauline communities, exhaustively documented yet primarily intended for the general but serious reader.

Reicke, Bo. *The New Testament Era: The World of the Bible from 500 B.C. to A.D. 100*. Philadelphia: Fortress, 1968. Extensive historical and political background in readable style and manageable length.

Theissen, Gerd. *The Social Setting of Pauline Christianity: Essays on Corinth*. Translation and introduction by John Schütz. Philadelphia: Fortress, 1982. Collected translations of several key articles first published in German, providing new social perspectives on composition and tensions of the Corinthian community.

Theissen, Gerd. *The Sociology of Early Palestinian Christianity*. Philadelphia: Fortress, 1978. Systematic study of the social structures and functions of the first Christians in Palestine in the years closest to the time of Jesus.

Verner, David C. *The Household of God: The Social World of the Pastoral Epistles*. Chico, CA: Scholars, 1983. A helpful scholarly study of the Pastorals in the light of the Hellenistic household.